Hot Chocolate
with God

Camryn Kelly

with Jill and Erin Kelly

Hot Chocolate with God

Just Me & Who God Created Me to Be

FaithWords

New York • Boston • Nashville

All Scripture quotations, unless otherwise indicated, are taken from THE HOLY
BIBLE, NEW INTERNATIONAL VERSION®. NIV®. Copyright © 1973, 1978, 1984 by Biblica,
Inc™. Used by permission of Zondervan. All rights reserved.
Scripture quotations marked NKJV are taken from the New King James
Version®. Copyright © 1982 by Thomas Nelson, Inc. Used by permission. All
rights reserved.
Scripture quotations marked *The Message* are taken from *The Message*.
Copyright © 1993, 1994, 1995, 1996, 2000, 2001, 2002 by NavPress Publishing
Group. Used by permission. All rights reserved.

FaithWords
Hachette Book Group
237 Park Avenue
New York, NY 10017

www.faithwords.com

Printed in the United States of America

First Edition: September 2011
10 9 8 7 6 5 4 3 2

FaithWords is a division of Hachette Book Group, Inc.
The FaithWords name and logo are trademarks of Hachette Book Group, Inc.

The publisher is not responsible for websites (or their content) that are not
owned by the publisher.

Library of Congress Cataloging-in-Publication Data
Kelly, Camryn, 1999–
    Hot chocolate with God : just me & who God created me to be / Camryn Kelly
with Jill and Erin Kelly. — 1st ed.
        p. cm.
    ISBN 978-0-89296-845-9
    1. Self-confidence—Religious aspects—Christianity—Juvenile literature.
2. Security (Psychology)—Juvenile literature. I. Kelly, Jill, 1969– II. Kelly, Erin,
1995– III. Title.
    BV4598.23.K45 2011
    248.8'2—dc22

                          2011007429

This amazing book is dedicated to all the girls out there

who want to live a life that honors God...

by just being who God created them to be.

This super Sweet and totally

Cool book belongs to:

Kiera Verness

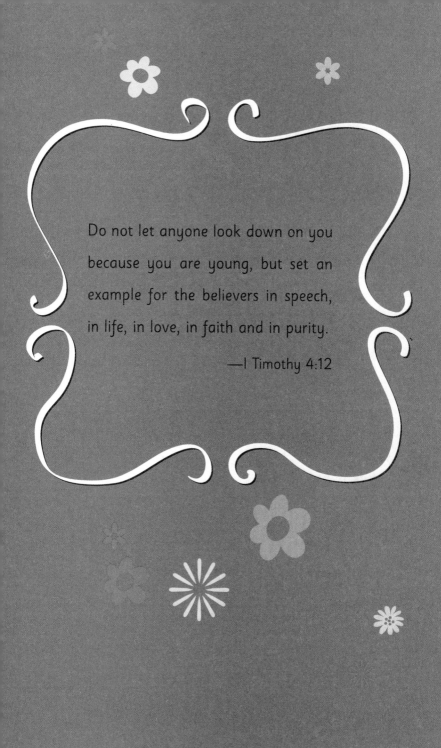

Do not let anyone look down on you because you are young, but set an example for the believers in speech, in life, in love, in faith and in purity.

—I Timothy 4:12

Thank you...

Bailey and Kiley Rush—You both know how much time we spent creating this book together. A lot. I love you both so much! Writing *Hot Chocolate with God* would not have been as much fun without you. I always have such a blast whenever I'm with you.

Shelby Rush—I'm so thankful that you were able to help with this very important project! You are so funny and creative, and I thought the questions you came up with were great.

Kim and Paige Waggoner—Aunt Kim and Paige, I love you both so much. *Hot Chocolate with God* is great because of your help. I loved all of your questions and comments.

Patti Thomas—You're so funny and we all love you. (Especially me!) Your goofy additions were perfect. Thank you for helping us.

Jessica Ohlson—I'm very thankful that you were able to take the time to share your heart with us. You're an amazing artist! I love your drawings and ideas for Cam, and I love you and your family.

Rick Kern—Wow, it's a good thing you're my mom's writing and editing buddy. *Hot Chocolate with God* could not have been done without you, that's for sure. You know all the editing stuff that we are clueless about. I'm so thankful for your help!

The FaithWords team—We love you, Jana. It was so much fun getting to know you during my mom's book tour in New York City. Now we get to be with you for *Hot Chocolate with God*, which is very exciting. I'm sure a lot of people that I'll never meet worked on this project—to all of those people, I say a big thank-you.

Mr. Robert Wolgemuth—Thank you for believing in my writing. I'm so grateful for all of your help. I hope you share this with your granddaughters.

To my mom and sister, Erin—We did it! *HCWG* is our project. I'm so thankful that we got to work on this together as a family. God is so awesome! I love you more…more… more!

Finally, I'd like to thank *Jesus*—I'm Your girl! Thank You for loving me just the way I am. *Hot Chocolate with God* is all Yours!

Contents

First of All . . .

Let's get something clear right from the start. You have enough to read with all the schoolwork that you're responsible for (unless you're reading this during the summer, which would be very cool—good for you). You need to know one very important thing—this is not just another book. *Hot Chocolate with God* is more than a book. It's more than an adventure. It's more than a journal or diary. This book is *you*. It's your heart! It's your journey.

With me, of course!

I can't let you do this on your own. Besides, I really want to come along for the ride.

I'm serious.

I hope that if I share my heart and journey with you, you'll share your heart with me. Obviously, I can't actually be with you (but maybe I'll meet you someday, and that would totally rock). But through sharing here and connecting on the *Hot Chocolate with God* website (which is so cool that I absolutely know you'll love it), we will get to know each other.

This book is packed full of fun stuff for you, but better than all that, I think this journey will change your life. I'm not exactly sure how, but I really hope that God will bless you through *Hot Chocolate with God*. He loves you more than I ever could, even more than your parents. He has a plan in all of this and it's good—very, very good.

So let's do this!

Grab a cool pen and let's get started. I prefer the sparkly, colorful kind. I drive my mother crazy over pens. No matter what store we go to, I NEED more pens—and notebooks!

I'll meet you on every page. Most of what you'll find here is very fun, real-life stuff. But some of what I'll share with you from my journey might be sort of embarrassing, scary, and at times sad. But that's life—it's a roller coaster of many ups and downs. Hang on, girlfriends!

I'm so excited!

I can hardly wait!

Oh, and one more thing, believe it or not, I've asked my mom and older sister, Erin, to join us. Yeah, I know, moms and teenage sisters can get on your nerves sometimes. Trust me, I know. But I needed my mom's help since she is a real writer and she's fun (most of the time). And Erin… Well, she's older and she's already lived through the "tween" years so she understands more than I do (I think). Even though she aggravates me to no end sometimes, I love her so much, and she's very smart and creative.

Ready?

Me too!

Thanks for taking this journey with me.

With love and excitement,

Camryn ("Cam")

P.S. You rock!

What You Need to Know . . .

Okay, so there are a few things you need to know before we get started.

1. This is yours! I've set this book up in sections, but you can do what you want. Jump and skip around (not on the book of course, because you might rip it or something). If you're like me, you'll want to fill in every single blank in order. But you don't have to. Do what you want!

2. I go by my nickname Cam throughout this book. You'll find *Cam Jam*, *Cam Fam*, and other fun things about me scattered here and there as you read. I'm me, and no one in the entire world can be me. When I share my heart with you, you might feel the same way I do, or you might not. And that's okay, because you and I are different. Just be yourself and have fun.

3. Throughout this book you will be invited to visit the *Hot Chocolate with God* website (**www.hotchocolatewithgod.com**) to view **Cam Clips**. My friends and I had so much fun putting these videos together. I know you'll love them. Every time you see a **Cam Clip**, there will be a special code word that you will need. When you go to the *Hot Chocolate* website **Cam Clips** section you will need

these special codes to view the fun videos. You're smart, so I know you'll be able to figure it out.

Get your parents involved. Did I really just say that? UGH! Yes, I did. I have to ask my parents if I can get on the Internet every time I use the computer. *"Every time?"* Yes, every time. There's a lot of junk on the Internet and I want to stay far away from all of it. So if you want to check out all the cool stuff on the *Hot Chocolate with God* website, you need to ask your mom or dad if it's okay. Got that? Don't try to sneak without asking, like I have before—bad choice.

4. As you take this journey, you will read **SWEET TRUTHS**. These are words from God's book—the Bible. I love reading the Bible! If you have no clue about the Bible, that's okay. Just as I have something to share with you and you have cool things to share with me, God wants to share His heart too. We know God's heart through His Word. You'll see. I think you'll really love hearing what God has to say.

5. Lastly, SHARE! You are amazing! Go into *your home,* neighborhood, school, and church—wherever. Go and share *you*! Share *your* journey and *your* heart with others, like *I* have with *you.*

Sweet Section 1

This Is Me...This Is My Life!

I will probably say this to you more times than I can count (hmmm, maybe my mom is rubbing off on me)—*YOU are special!*

You're chosen! You're like no one else on the face of this big huge Earth.

You are the only YOU ever created! This is amazing, incredible news!

If *you* really *believe* this and *live* like it's true, your life will rock.

I'm serious!

Your life is a *story*.

Everything about you forms a special story that no one else can tell but you. I know that sometimes you might wish your life were different, that you were different. But know this, you really are beautifully and wonderfully made. You are exactly YOU!

Are you ready to get into this or what?

Let's start with 100 questions only for you—because *only you can be you!* (And the cool thing is someone else might know the answers to these questions about you, but they can't ever be you.

Don't you even think about skipping some of these—it's time to spill the beans, my friends! Besides, these questions are too fun. Simple ones first, of course—get the easy questions out of the way. If you need help with some of these, go get it. (Remember, you can always send us a message or question through the website.) I can't wait to meet you someday, because I already like you so much. I know, that may seem odd, but it's true.

100 of the BEST Questions in the Entire World...All About You

1. First of all, what is today's date? (Every day is special—especially today, because you're having fun with me and *Hot Chocolate with God*.)

2. What are your first, middle, and last names, and nickname?

3. Who decided on your name?

Cam Jam: Believe it or not, my dad named my brother, my sister, and me. My mom doesn't know why she let my dad pick our names, but she loves his choices.

4. If you could change your name, what would you change it to, and why?

Cam Jam: Your name is important! You may not like the name your mom and dad chose to give you, but it's your special name. When you were born your name was officially written on a document called a birth certificate. Although many other people may have the same name that you do, only you are you. Your name is important because it's yours.

5. Two favorite girls' names?

    1.

    2.

6. Two favorite boys' names?

    1.

    2.

7. Use your first name to create an acrostic poem that describes you. Here's my example. Use the space next to my name to create your own poem.

C —cool, or candy "luver," since I love, love, love candy

A —adventurous

M —marvelous

R —royal

Y —young

N —nice

Cam Jam: You might be wondering why I chose *royal* for the letter *R*. Well, here's the deal. God says in His Word, the Bible, that I am His child, part of His family. He is the King and I am His young princess—so that makes me royalty. No, I don't live in a castle or wear a crown (I will in heaven, but that's another story for another time). But I'm His, and that makes me a princess. If you're His, you're royalty too.

8. Birth date and age right now?

9. What age do you look forward to turning, and why this age?

10. What **four things** would you like to do before you turn 14?

     1.

     2.

     3.

     4.

11. What do you want for your birthday this year?

12. Do you share the same birthday with anyone else in your family or anyone else you know? If you do, who?

Cam Jam: My daddy and brother have the exact same birthday—Valentine's Day, February 14. I'll tell you more about them later.

A bunch of baby stuff...

Cam Jam: Okay—I have to tell you something really quick. These next questions are about when you were born. Yes, the baby stuff. I know you don't remember what happened when you were born. No one remembers that stuff. So you might have to ask your parents about some of this. It's good to know the answers to these questions. It's your history and it matters.

13. Weight and height at birth?

Cam Jam: I know there must be tons of pictures of you around your house. Maybe your mom has a special box where she keeps the family photos. See if you can find a baby picture of yourself as well as a recent photo. Do you recognize yourself as a baby? Please make sure you ask your mom if you can use these photos for this book.

Me as an adorable baby . . .

That's me today.

14. Did you have a lot of hair when you were born or were you bald? (I'm cracking up right now.)

15. Hair color when you were born—and right now? (I think it's really weird that our hair color changes over time without us even going to the salon to get it colored—hmmm, why?)

16. Eye color?

17. Who else in your family has the same eye color that you have?

18. Are you having fun answering these questions? (Hee-hee, just wondering.)

19. What time were you born?

20. Where were you born? (Like, what state, city, and hospital?)

21. Where do you live right now? (Write down your full address.)

Cam Jam: Did you know that God determined exactly where you would live? He decided long before you were born that you would live where you live with your family right now. He knows the name of your street. He knows the name of your town or city. Isn't that incredible? Best of all, He knows *your* name!

And He determined the times set for them and the exact places where they should live. God did this so that men would seek Him and perhaps reach out for Him and find Him, though He is not far from each one of us. For in Him we live and move and have our being. (Acts 17:26–28)

22. Do you live in the country, the city, a town, or a village? Describe where you live.

23. Do you live near the ocean or mountains? If yes, which one?

24. Do you live anywhere near an anthill? Did you ever accidentally sit on it?

25. If you could live anywhere in the entire world, where would you live, and why?

26. When you were a baby or toddler, did you have a special blanket or stuffed animal? Did it have a name? Describe what it looked like.

Cam Jam: Be honest. I'm not afraid to say that I had a favorite blanket—we called it my "butterfly blankie." When I was a little kid, I would not go anywhere without it. I still have my butterfly blankie, and it's still as soft as ever. Maybe I'll save it so I can show it to my kids someday—if it lasts that long. My big sister, Erin, had a special blanket too. Her blanket was named "fruit blankie." Erin was very attached to her blanket (so I've heard). One time her fruit blankie was accidentally dropped into a lake. I wasn't even born when this happened, so obviously I wasn't there. My parents were on a boat and they were carrying my sister off the boat and her blanket fell into the lake. It went all the way to the very bottom. It was late at night, but there were lights where the boat was docked so you could see Erin's blanket sitting on the bottom of the lake. As you might imagine, my sissy was freaking out. With the help of my grandpa and a long fishhook, my dad was able to rescue fruit blankie. So blankie and Erin lived happily ever after. Seriously, she still has fruit blankie. It's falling apart, but it will always be special to Erin.

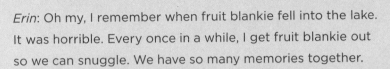

Erin: Oh my, I remember when fruit blankie fell into the lake. It was horrible. Every once in a while, I get fruit blankie out so we can snuggle. We have so many memories together.

27. Did you suck your thumb or a pacifier? (This question is for when you were little, and you better not have a pacifier now—yikes. I was a "passy" girl, and Mommy had a very hard time breaking me from my pacifier. Come to think of it, that is probably why I have braces right now.)

28. How many baby teeth do you still have?

29. How many horse teeth do you have? (Ba-ha-ha, I hope none!)

30. Where is the weirdest place where you lost a baby tooth?

31. Have you ever had any cavities?

32. One more little kid question, and don't be embarrassed at all by this: Have you ever peed the bed or your pants? (Lots of kids do, even my dad used to when he was little, so don't worry about it. You're not the only kid in the world to do this. In fact, I bet every single kid in the world has peed the bed or their pants at least once.)

Okay, enough with the baby blabbing,
let's talk about you now as a
sweet tween girl.

33. Do you like to dance?

34. Have you ever taken dance lessons? If you have, what type of dance lessons did you take (hip-hop, jazz, ballet, etc.)?

35. Do you like to sing?

Cam Jam: Here's the deal. I know a lot of songs by heart and I like to sing them whenever and wherever. It doesn't really matter to me if I don't have a good voice. I'll sing and dance if I want to. My family says that I have rhythm. In other words, I can dance. I've never taken dance lessons. Well, actually, I did take a few lessons with my sister and some friends but we all quit because all the songs they played were really bad—like, with inappropriate words and stuff. I've begged my mom to get me started in some sort of dance class. Hopefully I'll be getting some lessons very soon. I'll let you know when it happens. I really want to take hip-hop classes. We shall see.

36. Do you play some kind of musical instrument?

Cam Jam: P.S. Beating on your brother or little sister—or anyone else for that matter—like a drum doesn't count…Just saying!

37. What instrument(s) do you play?

38. Can you whistle?

39. What about art? Do you like to draw?

40. Do you collect anything? What kinds of things do you collect, and how many of your collectible things do you have?

Favorites: We all have favorite things. My favorites have changed over time. For instance, my favorite color used to be orange but now it's purple. My sister and I laugh because as soon as you tell my mom that a certain color is your favorite, everything she gets for you is that color. She's funny. So what are some of your favorites?

41. Favorite color?

42. Favorite number?

43. Favorite fruit and vegetable?

44. Favorite dessert?

45. **Top two** favorite snack foods?

    1.

    2.

46. Favorite candy?

47. Favorite potato chips?

48. Favorite cereal?

49. Which one is your favorite: whole milk, 2%, 1%, skim milk, chocolate milk, strawberry milk, goat's milk, almond milk, frog's milk, soy milk, or rice milk?

Cam Jam: Can you believe there are so many different kinds of milk to drink? Oh, and there's no such thing as frog's milk—at least I don't think there is. We sort of have a milk controversy in our family. My mom loves organic skim milk and my dad likes regular 1%. He thinks organic milk is too expensive. He's convinced that all the organic stuff is nonsense. Since my mother usually does all the grocery shopping, she buys the milk. But in order to keep the peace, my mom buys both kinds of milk—organic for her and regular 1% for my dad. Erin and I drink whatever we find in the refrigerator.

My aunt Kim says that milk is not good for you—that it's good for baby cows. What, is she crazy? She's, like, a holistic, organic type of person. I don't understand most of what she's talking about when she explains all the organic stuff. But I love her anyway. I think I'll stick to drinking regular 1% milk.

50. Do you know anyone like my aunt who eats only organic food?   Who?

51. Circle your favorite: dark chocolate, milk chocolate, white chocolate, orange chocolate, NO chocolate, or just give me ANY chocolate!

52. Favorite kind of cake?

Cam Jam: By the way, why do older people say, "You can't have your cake and eat it too"? What does that even mean? Ask an older person and write their answer here.

53. Favorite ice cream?

54. Favorite fast food restaurant, and what do you usually eat there?

55. Favorite utensil? (Hmm, spoon . . . fork? I bet you never thought about this question before—yeah, I told you this book was cool.)

56. Favorite flower?

Cam Jam: My cousin Ben knows a lot about flowers, trees, and fish. He's a nature boy. I'm amazed that he knows as much as he does. God has really given him a love for all that He has created. We should appreciate nature and all that God has made for us to enjoy. When we take the time to stop, look, and smell the different flowers and trees and creatures (I suppose I wouldn't like to smell the creatures), I think we would be amazed too, just like my cousin Benjamin.

57. Favorite store(s)? Yeah, you might have more than one favorite, like I do.

Cam Jam: I love Target, Justice, and Office Max. Yes, Office Max, because I LOVE pens! And notebooks too.

58. Favorite book?

Cam Jam: Since my mom is a bestselling author— so cool—let's interview my mom and find out more about all this writing stuff. She's written three books so far so I'm going to ask her about her books. I'd also like her to tell us what it is like to write a book. Like, is it hard? Is it ever boring? How long does it take? And how do you unblock writer's block? That kind of stuff. If you're interested in all of this, go to:

⦗J Cam Clips on the website (CODE: MOMMY).

59. Favorite television show?

60. Favorite movie?

61. What snack do you get when you go to the movies?

62. If you could star in one of your favorite movies, what movie would you be in, and what character would you play and why?

Time OUT! Let's do something different. Circle one of the two choices in *Take Your Pick*. Yes, these are just random questions, but it's fun—and you know it! I've added my opinion here and there in parentheses.

Take Your Pick

Walk in the woods	Stroll in the city (I'm not a city girl.)
Hamburger	Hot dog
Milk shake	Ice cream cone
Dog (as many as possible)	Cat (cute, but Grammie is allergic)
Jeans	Comfy in my sweats
Watch a movie	Read a book (I'm not a big reader, unless it's the Bible.)
Sleep in	Sleep in (hee-hee)
Breakfast	Dinner
One pillow	Lots of pillows and blankets
Unload the dishwasher	Clean up after dinner

Let's get back to the *100 Best Questions About You in the Entire World.*

63. Favorite Disney and Nickelodeon shows?

64. Favorite Animal Planet show?

65. Favorite animals? (List as many as you would like to.)

66. Wouldn't it have been so cool to have been on Noah's ark? Wait a minute: It probably smelled really bad. Forty days and forty nights on a boat with all those animals—yikes! What did Noah and his crew do about the poop and stuff? What would you have done? I would've lit some of the nice-smelling candles my mom has. What do you think it was like on Noah's Ark? I'd probably get stuck cleaning the stalls—GROSS!

67. If you could have a wild animal as a pet, which wild animal would you choose, and what would you name your pet?

68. Favorite celebrity, female and male?

Cam Jam: My favorite celeb is my dad, of course. He'll always be my favorite even though he makes me play basketball when I don't want to. My daddy used to play professional football for the Buffalo Bills. He was the quarterback, and he wore number 12. I'll explain more about my dad in a minute.

69. Imagine that you get to have a celebrity sleepover. What **two celebrities** would you invite to your slumber party?

    1.

    2.

70. What would you like to be famous or well known for in this world?

71. Favorite singer, female and male?

72. Favorite band?

73. Imagine this: You won the party of a lifetime. Invite all your friends and family because you get to select any three groups to come and perform a concert at the best party ever.
    What **three bands** would you pick for this absolutely over-the-top event?

    1.

    2.

    3.

74. Have you ever been to a concert?   Which ones have you been to?

75. Top **two songs** you listen to all the time?

    1.

    2.

76. Favorite Wii or video or computer game? Or list one of each.

Cam Jam: My favorite Wii game is *Just Dance*. I have to show you how hysterical and fun this game is. I'll have my friends Bailey and Kiley play too. Come and check it out at:

♪ Cam Clips on the website **(CODE: DANCE).**

77. Favorite board game?

78. Favorite amusement park ride?

79. Seriously, have you ever been on a roller coaster?

Did you get sick or ride it over and over again?

80. List all the fun places you've been to. (For example: Six Flags, Walt Disney World, etc.)

81. Have you ever been to a rodeo or circus or craft show?

82. Favorite hobby or hobbies?

83. Favorite sport?

84. List all the sports you have ever tried to play.

85. Favorite professional sport and sports team?

Cam Jam: I will never like a team more than the Buffalo Bills NFL football team. It's my dad's team and we will always cheer for them. Our family usually goes to the home games. We live, like, five minutes away from Ralph Wilson Stadium where the Buffalo Bills play. Check this out! Do you want to see the stadium where the team plays? With the help of my dad, I'm going to show you a real NFL stadium. I can hardly wait for you to see this. It's so cool! Let's go to:

cam Clips (CODE: FOOTBALL).

86. Have you ever been to a professional sports event, like an NBA (National Basketball Association) or NFL (National Football League) or maybe an NHL (National Hockey League) game?
What game, and who played?

Just a few more favorites...

87. Favorite holiday and why?

88. Favorite season and why?

89. Do you get a lot of snow in the winter where you live?

90. Okay, everyone has done this at least once. Have you ever eaten snow? (By the way, I hope the snow was white and not yellow. Trust me, that yellow stuff is bad for you.)

91. Who taught you how to swim, and how old were you when you learned?

92. Who taught you how to ride a bike?
How old were you?

Cam Jam: If you don't know how to ride a bike or swim, don't feel bad—everything isn't for everybody. But if you decide you want to learn, I'm sure someone can help you.

93. When you can drive, what car would you like to drive (make, model, and color)?

Is this your favorite vehicle?

94. Top five favorite things?

1.

2.

3.

4.

5.

Camryn's Favorite Things Word Search

```
X I O J U K L N B R T N E J S
E T A L O C O H C T O H C X E
R Q I A Y E O T K Z N C N Z I
U E P M G D Y N Y E K T A P R
Q J G B L A N K E T S I D O R
V I O N I T N A D W P K I Y E
D W N U I S S Q C A U Z K W B
T B A G R F O E U O R Q U R P
N I E E J N R H M V P S V Y S
Z R Z H B P A E K H L O V U A
S E A I E U O L T E E S Y A R
B W S K H G U W S T N O B R I
W F Z I H W B H B E U M L N J
U E H Z P Q H V P M W B D W A
R C E L B I B B L N Z Y O C N
```

BIBLE	BLANKETS	BUTTERFINGER
CANDY	CHIHUAHUA	DANCE
HOT CHOCOLATE	JOURNALS	PENS
PURPLE	RASPBERRIES	TIGERS

Really Quick...Five Quick, Silly Random Questions About You

1. Have you ever gone bowling?

2. Have you ever seen a shooting star?

3. Weirdest place you've ever fallen asleep?

4. Do you know how to do a load of laundry? If you don't, why don't you ask your mom to show you how?

5. Has a bird ever pooped on you? Where did you get hit?

I have a feeling you liked *Take Your Pick*, so here's some more. Get to it, girlfriend!

Text my friends	Make a phone call
Quiet night at home	Hanging with friends at a party
Clean freak	Messy Marvin
Right-handed	Lefty and lovin' it (that's me)
Ponytail	Let my hair down
Uniform	Wear what you want
Hot Chocolate with God	Get stung by a bee (LOL!!!)
Pet spider (no—never)	Pet snake
Shower	Bath with lots of bubbles
Clean your room	Take the garbage out

Okay, let's tackle (my dad was a quarterback—what can I say?) the rest of the *100 Best Questions About You in the Entire World.*

95. What are **three fun and unique things** about you? List them.

1.

2.

3.

96. What are all the different places you have visited (states, countries)? List them.

97. If you could travel to a foreign country, what country would you pick and why?

98. Do you get an allowance?

99. Congratulations! You were just given one million dollars. What are you going to do with the money?

100. Have you ever donated any of your own money to charity?

Cam Jam: I'm so excited to tell you about this. Our family started a charity foundation named after my brother, Hunter, called the Hunter's Hope Foundation. This foundation was started when my brother was just eight months old (of course, I wasn't even born yet). Through Hunter's Hope we are helping so many children who are suffering with the same disease my brother had. I'll tell you all about him in the family section. Actually, I'll tell you about him in this **Cam Clip** too. I'm going to take you on a tour of the Hunter's Hope Foundation. You'll actually be able to meet my grandma. She runs the foundation and she is amazing. I love her so much. I'll have her tell you all about what we do at Hunter's Hope. Come with me and I'll share with you what's very special and important to our entire family. Go to:

Cam Clips (CODE: HOPE).

This Is Me...This Is My Life
Double Puzzle

NUEIUQ

☐☐☐☐☐☐
13　11　9

PAILECS

☐☐☐☐☐☐☐
　　　4

UDWFLEORN

☐☐☐☐☐☐☐☐☐
　2　　5

HATFI

☐☐☐☐☐
8

PUTRIY

☐☐☐☐☐☐
　　10　1

LOEDV

☐☐☐☐☐
14　　6

PUPREOS

☐☐☐☐☐☐☐
　3

LEIF

☐☐☐☐
12　7

☐☐☐　☐☐☐　B☐☐☐☐☐☐☐☐
1 2 3　4 5 6　7 8 9 10 11 12 13 14

Unscramble each of the clue words that describe you in some way. Copy the letters in the numbered squares to the other squares at the bottom with the same number. Have FUN!!

42

Sweet Section 2

Freckles, Bras, Makeup, and Everything Else Body and Beauty

Warning! This chapter might get a little goofy and uncomfortable.

But fear not! Cam is here to laugh with you through this very mysterious thing called the tween body.

It's a good thing I have an older sister. Erin has been a living example for me of what I can expect as I continue to grow. Yikes! I sure hope I don't get those mood swings like she gets sometimes. (*Erin*: Wow, Cam, thanks. Come on, Sissy. Give me a break here. You just wait until you're a teenager. Then we'll see what you have to say about all this.) I'm not my sister, so even though we are in the same family, we are growing and developing in different ways. But before we get into all that, let's talk about YOU.

You are unique! No one on the face of the earth is like you. No one can be you. I know I've already said this before, but it's worth repeating. You are the only *you* God has ever and will ever create. Isn't that amazing? In all of history there was never anyone who looked exactly like you. Today, you will not find another person on the globe who thinks the thoughts you do. From this day forward until forever, there will never be another human being with your fingerprints, nose shape, or body. Plain and simple—there will never ever be another *you*. No one can take your place! Wow!

Check this out! I know you probably look in the mirror often throughout the day, like I do. What do you see? I'm not a teenager yet, like my sister, but it seems the older you get the more you check yourself out. My sister isn't boy crazy like a lot of girls her age (thank God), but I've noticed that she cares more about how she looks whenever she knows there might be some cute boys around. (And that's a whole other story for later.)

(*Erin:* I don't look in the mirror more because of cute boys. Give me a break, Camryn. There's nothing wrong with wanting to look good, Sissy.)

To be honest with you, sometimes I don't like what I see in the mirror.

Go and stand in front of the mirror and list **three things** you like most about your outer appearance.

1.

2.

3.

Go grab one of your parents or someone you love and have them look in the mirror with you. Ask this person to tell you **three things** they see when they look at you in the mirror.

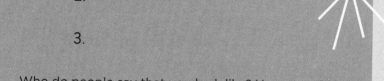

1.

2.

3.

Who do people say that you look like? Your mom? Your dad? Maybe your grandma or grandpa?

Cam Jam: Some of my relatives (including my mother—I'll have to talk to her about this) say that I look like my dad did when he was a kid. I think it's the freckles, because I don't think I look anything like my dad. Come on, people!

While we're talking about it, do you have freckles?

Do you wish you were taller or shorter—or are you happy with your height?

How tall are you right now? Ask an adult to measure you.

How much do you weigh?

How much does your mom weigh? (On second thought, you better not ask her. Move on to the next question.)

Do you wish you weighed more or less?

Cam Jam: Most girls are obsessed with their weight. Why? Is it because all the girls on the covers of magazines are so skinny? Most of those magazines are totally computerized (in other words, what you see is not what's real. Most magazine images are changed by using special computer techniques.) We all have different body shapes. If we use the skinny people or magazine cover chicks as a body standard we'll never be happy with our own body shape. I think this is a serious problem for some girls. It might be a serious issue right now for you. Let's do this: Use this piece of journal paper to talk to God about how you feel about your body right now. Be honest! Tell Him exactly how you feel. He made you. He designed the shape of your body. God wants you to know how wonderfully made you are in every way.

Describe your hair. Is it curly? (Like mine—UGH!!) Straight? Long or short?

What's your favorite hairstyle?

How do you wear your hair most of the time?

Oh my, did you ever cut your own hair?

Do you ever straighten or curl your hair?

Cam Jam: This is a great story I absolutely must tell you. We were reading this section to my grandma and she started talking about what it was like when she was a teenager. My grandma (my mom's mom) had eight sisters and two brothers—whoa! Her family couldn't afford to buy real curlers for the girls to fancy up their hair so my grandma said they had to use socks to curl their hair. Socks? Yes, can you believe it? We were laughing our heads off as my grammie shared how she and her sisters would roll their wet hair up in socks. They would all go to bed with a head full of socks. I wonder if they had enough socks for all those sisters? I'll have to ask my grandma.

When we started talking about straightening our hair, my grandma had another hysterical but true story. Because they didn't have straighteners way back when she was a kid, my grammie and her sisters had to do something I would suggest you and I NEVER do. My grandma and her sisters would flatten their hair by using a *real* iron (yes, the kind your mom uses to iron your clothes!). She said they would lay their hair on the ironing board and iron it. WHAT?! When she told us this story we couldn't stop laughing. And we were all, like, "Are you crazy, Grandma?" A word to the wise—don't ever try this at home, or ANYWHERE!

What's your favorite shampoo and conditioner?

Cam Jam: Okay, here's my deal with hair and height. First of all, my shampoo and conditioner must smell like fruit or flowers. Some shampoos smell so gross, which only means that my hair will end up smelling like that too. No, thanks—I don't know about you but stinky hair doesn't work for me. Most of the time, my hair drives me crazy! I have naturally very wavy hair (notice I didn't say curly—don't call my hair curly, ummm yeah). I usually straighten my hair with a straightener, which takes forever. And when I'm rushing to get ready for school, the hair-straightening thing doesn't go over real well with my dad. My dad just doesn't understand because, well, I hate to say it but he doesn't have a lot of hair. But that's okay, because I love him anyway. And no matter how much you and I fuss with our outer appearance, God loves us anyway. He made us girls so He knows how we like to fuss.

Lately, I've been trying to enjoy having wavy hair. LOL. I'm getting very adventurous with scrunching, and believe it or not, I'm starting to like my waves (as long as they don't wave good-bye—HA!).

As far as my height is concerned, I always hear my mom say how "long" I am. So I guess that means I'm tall for my age. Speaking of long, not too long ago, I had to get a physical for school. Of course, it was no fun at all because I had to get a shot. In fact, the doctor tried to convince my mom that I should get three shots but I kept giving my mom the look of dread and fear. Thankfully, she heard my unspoken looks and I ended up getting only one shot. When the doctor measured me, I was 5 feet 5 inches. (By the time this book is published, I'm sure I'll be over 6 feet tall. I'll be old and gray by then too. Just kidding—but I will surely be taller than I am now while writing this.) Compared to the other kids in my grade, I'm tall and long. But I'm cool with my height, because I'm the perfect height for me. And you are the perfect height for you.

When was the last time you had a physical exam?

Did you have to get any shots?

Do you usually cry when you get shots?

More cool stuff about YOU...

Since we've never met, if we were to have a telephone conversation and I asked you to describe what you look like, what would you say?

Since we're talking about talking to each other over the phone, I'm curious: Do you have a cell phone?

What kind?   How about a mobile phone?

HA! They are the same thing—gotcha! If you do have a cell phone, who pays your bill?

Don't wait, go and thank the person who pays your cell phone bill right now.

Who texts (calls) you the most and who do you text (call) the most?

What's your dream phone, the phone you've always wanted?

 Design It:

Get creative and design your own cell phone case.

Do you have long or short nails?

Do you bite your nails? (If you do, STOP it—right now. ☺ Don't feel bad, because I sometimes bite my nails too.)

Do you have nail polish on right now?   If yes, what color?

Favorite nail polish color?

Have you ever had a manicure?

Have you ever had a pedicure?

Have you ever accidently kicked the person giving you a pedicure because your feet are so ticklish you couldn't help it?

Are you ticklish?   If you answered yes, where are you ticklish? (Don't worry, I won't tell anyone…)

Do you have braces?   If you do, what color bands do you have right now?

How long have you had your braces on?

How long did your orthodontist say that you would have to wear your braces? Do they hurt?

Cam Jam: I have braces and it's really not so bad. I have blue, pink, yellow, and purple bands on right now. And here's something not very many people know…my mother had braces put on when she was 40 years old. Are you kidding me? NO—it's true, and she didn't even tell any of us that she was going to have them put on, not even my dad. It was shocking and hysterical the day we all found out. My mother picked us up at school as usual and when we got in the car she looked at my sister, Erin, and me and smiled really big. We both freaked out. I think Erin was embarrassed because the first thing she said was, "Mom, you're forty years old. You can't have braces." After the initial shock wore off I thought it was pretty cool that my mom had braces. I even asked her if she would get colored bands to match me. She didn't go for that suggestion. She only wore clear bands. That's so boring. I was glad that my mom could sort of relate to me. She only had to wear her braces for six months. I still have braces and I'm not supposed to get them off until I'm in ninth grade. Oh well. At least I'll have nice straight teeth when this is all said and done. By the way, braces or no braces, I'm beautiful because God made me. And you're beautiful too. Don't ever forget it!

Do you wear glasses or contacts? If you wear glasses, what do they look like?

Do you have a birthmark? (I do.) If you do, where is it?

Do you think you're *beautiful*?

When you hear someone say the word *beautiful*, what's the first thing that pops into your mind?

Cam Jam: First of all, you're beautiful! I want you to go and find a 3 x 5-inch card or a small piece of paper and your favorite color marker. On this piece of paper I want you to write the following in all caps:

I AM BEAUTIFULLY MADE!

NO ONE IN THE ENTIRE WORLD IS LIKE ME.

I AM BEAUTIFUL IN EVERY WAY.

GOD LOVES ME JUST THE WAY I AM!

After you're finished writing the above message, find some tape and put this piece of paper on whatever mirror you look into most of the time. (You might have to ask your mom if it's okay to put tape on the mirror. It's always good to check with her.) I hope that you read this message every day—many times a day. Why? Because it's true! If anyone tells you something different, they're lying to you. I'm so serious. We can't look in the mirror and think about what other people think of us. We need to look in the mirror and believe what you wrote on that card. Let's make a promise to each other (ummm, I guess I should ask this first, are you a good promise keeper?). Let's read our beauty reminder card out loud every morning for a week straight. Okay? Do you think you can do it? Remember, it doesn't matter what other people say or think. What matters is what God says and thinks about you—and He thinks you're beautiful, and that's all there is to it.

I praise You because I am fearfully and wonderfully made; Your works are wonderful, I know that full well. (Psalm 139:14)

Have you ever played dress up with your mom's clothes and shoes?

What outfit would you wear every single day if you could?

Erin: When I read this, I started cracking up. When I was Cam's age, I used to wear this *Jesus Rocks* T-shirt almost every single day. I wore it so much that my mom eventually purchased, like, five more of the exact same shirt so that she didn't have to wash the same one every day. It was such a cute T-shirt, but I eventually got over wearing it all the time. Just like I eventually stopped doing the "wearing the exact same outfit as your best friend" thing. Ummm yeah. When

I look at pictures of my friend Shelby and me dressed like twins, I just shake my head and wonder why my mother let us do that. Oh well, I guess it was a tween thing.

So what about you? Do you and your best friend ever dress in matching outfits?

Do you try to wear clothes that are "in style"?

Cam Jam: The whole style thing drives me crazy. It's always changing. What's cool today might not be cool a few months from now. Ridiculous. Of course, I like to wear cute outfits but I don't really care if what I'm wearing is not "in style." As far as I'm concerned, whatever I wear is in style for me. I love cute clothes (and purses—can't forget the accessories), but I'd much rather be comfortable. Yes, comfort is key for me. My sissy is the same way. She doesn't get all caught up in the fashionista thing either. She has a very casual style that consists of sweatpants and T-shirts most of the time. She's a great example for me because she isn't boy crazy or style crazy.

My mother is the "fashion police," or should I say the Momma Clothes Monitor (or Monster, ha-ha). She determines whether or not what my sister Erin and I have on is appropriate. The "hallelujah test" is a great way for us to make sure whether the shirt we have on is long enough. What's the hallelujah test? I'm glad you asked. Go and stand in front of a mirror. Raise both of your hands straight up into the air above your head, and as you're doing this say "hallelujah." If your shirt rides up high above your waist, exposing your cute little belly button, it's too short. That's the test. Did you pass or fail? As soon as my shirts start to get a little too short for me I give them to my cousin Paige or my friend Kiley. No sense keeping them if I can't wear them again, right?

Speaking of belly buttons, do you have an "innie" or an "outtey"? (I don't think you'll find belly button lingo in the dictionary, so that's my spelling of the two words. Oh, and I have an innie, sort of.)

Favorite shoes?

Oh yeah, by the way, what is your shoe size?

What's your dog's shoe size? (Ha-ha-ha-ha...I crack myself up.)

Cam Jam: Let me tell you about my shoe size. Okay, this is crazy. My mom is a size 9 and the last time I bought shoes, they were a size 9. What?!!! My sister is a size 10, but she's, like, 16. Why do I have such big feet? All the better to dance around the house with—right?! Or maybe it runs in the family. Believe it or not, my older cousin, Brian, wears a size 15 shoe. What in the world?! I didn't know they made shoes that big.

Do you have pierced ears?

How old were you when you had your ears pierced?

Do you like to wear jewelry?

Do you carry a purse?

What does your favorite purse look like?

Do you wear perfume?

What's your favorite perfume?

Are you allowed to wear makeup?

If yes, what do you wear?

Cam Jam: I love makeup and I think it's a lot of
fun to wear. My mom doesn't allow my sister and me to
wear too much makeup, which is fine with me because I
like a very natural look anyway. If you're not old enough
or allowed to wear makeup right now, that's totally cool.
Obeying and honoring your parents and their choices for
you is far more important than wearing makeup. Yeah—for
sure. Besides, you might choose to never wear makeup and
that's cool too, because you're beautiful just the way you
are.

What's your favorite lip-gloss flavor?

Put lipstick on and leave a lip print right here: SWAK—
Sealed With A Kiss.

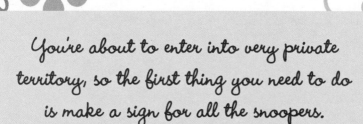

You're about to enter into very private territory, so the first thing you need to do is make a sign for all the snoopers.

Fill in the sign below with whatever you want to say in order to keep other readers *OUT*! (Mine would read: *BEWARE!! No sisters or boys allowed.*)

_____

_____

Do you have little "buds" or "M&M's"—otherwise known as boobies?

Cam Jam: Why am I asking you this question when it makes me embarrassed just thinking about it? Well, it's part of life. It's part of growing into the beautiful woman that God is creating. Mom tells me that everybody grows according to their own timetable. You might not develop at the same time as your friends because your body has its own special timetable. God knows exactly what's going on with your body, and it will grow at the rate that is perfect for you. Isn't this good news?! Your body is unique to you and you have no control over when you will get boobies and all that growing girl stuff. So don't compare yourself to other girls.

Do you wear a bra yet? _____ If yes, what size and color?

Have you had any zits yet?

Cam Jam: Ugh! I can't stand pimples or zits—whatever you want to call them. They're so gross. My mother always wants to help me with mine. In other words, she wants to torture me by squeezing my zits for me. Disgusting! I can do it on my own, thank you. We all get pimples and have to deal with them. I wash my face at least two times a day, if not more. I try not to pick my face too much but sometimes I just have to. Usually, the more I pick, the more I find, and that's not good so I try not to be too consumed with what's happening on my face.

Erin: Yeah, Mom used to try and help me with my zits too, Cam. Eventually, I guess I got fast enough to escape so she stopped trying. Either that or I figured out how to do it all on my own. Don't worry, you'll learn too.

Please don't freak out with this next question! Do you have your period yet?

Cam Jam: Let's get serious for a minute. If there's something that I've asked you that you don't understand or haven't learned yet, that's just fine. The best thing to do is talk to your mother about it. You're learning and growing, just like me. We're not going to fully understand everything, so it's important to ask questions. Don't ever be afraid to ask questions—even the embarrassing ones, like these. Remember, the only silly question is the one you don't ask—my mom says that, and I think it's true.

Are you uncomfortable with the changes happening to your body right now?

Do you use deodorant?　　　If so, what kind?

Do you shave your legs and underarms yet?

If you shave, how often do you have to do it?

Cam Jam: Well, this is sort of funny but not so funny. I begged and bugged my mom to let me shave my legs. I bugged her until she finally let me do it. Well, I didn't actually do it; my mom shaved my legs for me. We got everything all set up in my bathtub: shaving cream, a soft towel to sit on, and a razor. My friends Bailey and Kiley were there for support. Let me tell you, I freaked out the whole time. Of course I didn't kick or anything since I would've gotten cut, but I was so scared. Once it was all said and done and my legs were silky smooth, oddly, I didn't like how my legs felt. My mother had explained that my legs would feel very different without hair, but I didn't understand what she meant until I experienced it myself. Well, I haven't shaved my legs since. I know I'll eventually have to, but I'm going to wait. You should wait for as long as you can too. Trust me, it's no big deal, and besides you'll have the rest of your life to shave. Stay unshaven for as long as you can, girlfriend!

Do you take a bath or shower?

Do you usually eat three meals a day?

What do you like for breakfast?

Do you do a lot of snacking during the day?

What do you usually grab to snack on?

If you could eat only one food for the rest of your life, what would it be, and why did you pick this food?

Do you drink a lot of water?

Do you take vitamins every day?

Do you exercise?

How often do you exercise?

Have you ever had stitches?   Where?
What happened?

Did you ever break a bone?   Which one?
What happened?

Did you ever have to spend the night in the hospital?
What happened?

Have you ever been to the emergency room? What happened?

How many hours of sleep do you usually get each night?

What do you usually sleep with every night?

How often do you brush your teeth?

What color is your toothbrush right now?

Do you floss?   How often?

Do you check your teeth for leftover food after you have eaten? (GROSS!!)

When you see food stuck in your friend's teeth do you tell her about it?

Cam Jam: A true friend always tells her BFF when she has junk stuck in her teeth. Oh, and you absolutely must tell when those nasty boogies start creeping out of your friend's nose. You don't want the boy she sits next to in class to tell her, do you? You absolutely, positively must rescue her from such embarrassment.

What You Need to Remember—
I-Post-its

These are what we'll call I-Post-its. They are little reminders for you…and for me. I've filled in some of them, but you can fill in the rest. Check it out!

I am wonderfully made!

Nothing can separate me from God's love!

 **Man looks at the outward appearance, but the LORD looks at the heart.**

(1 Samuel 16:7)

Men and women look at the face; GOD looks into the heart. *(The Message)*

Body and Beauty Word Search

```
H  S  U  L  C  C  M  H  H  A  H  A  K  X  A
T  S  A  G  U  I  Y  Q  G  O  P  A  H  G  R
M  C  Q  M  R  F  S  N  Y  Y  V  A  L  E  V
L  S  K  R  X  R  I  Y  A  T  E  W  U  G  C
U  W  O  W  K  G  O  T  K  Y  U  L  F  A  L
X  R  K  J  N  F  V  F  U  J  Y  A  R  M  O
E  C  N  A  R  A  E  P  P  A  K  F  E  I  T
G  Z  H  N  G  L  C  B  T  Q  E  A  D  B  H
X  C  T  L  N  R  A  T  S  E  V  B  N  G  E
E  U  Q  I  N  U  O  L  K  A  E  O  O  V  S
F  A  S  H  I  O  N  W  Y  Z  Z  D  W  J  W
H  X  D  I  P  Z  G  D  I  G  H  S  X  B  Y
Y  V  O  U  N  Y  O  D  P  N  V  E  A  L  Z
R  V  H  W  E  B  L  H  N  P  G  D  O  B  B
S  I  N  V  I  A  Z  W  D  Z  D  L  L  C  Y
```

APPEARANCE	BEAUTIFUL	BEAUTY
BODY	CHANGING	CLOTHES
FASHION	GROWING	IMAGE
MIRROR	UNIQUE	WONDERFUL

Sweet Section 3

What's on the Inside— Getting to the Heart of the Matter

I love the title of this chapter because what's on the inside, your heart, is all that really matters. You can be the most beautiful girl, but if your heart is filled with selfishness and rotten things then it doesn't even matter how beautiful you are on the outside. It's true! You can't radiate beauty on the outside if your heart's not in the right place. My mom always says, "Shine on, girl…let your light shine!" When she says this she's talking about shining the light of hope that we have in our hearts for all to see. That hope is Jesus! I have so much to say about Him, but it will have to wait. For now, let's talk about the real you, the person on the inside. You're not just a body walking around. You're a human being with a unique personality. Just as no one has the exact same body as you, no one has your personality. Your personality, the way you think, feel, act—all the amazing things on the inside that make you you—are who YOU *really* are. Again, as I've said before, no one can be YOU. You're the only You ever created. So what's on the inside? Let's talk about it.

You and Your Personality—The You on the Inside

They say you can tell a lot about someone by their handwriting (hmm, I'm not so sure about that). Practice your autograph right here.

Cam Jam: When my daddy was growing up he would practice his autograph all the time. His dream was to become a professional football player and that dream came true. My dad told me that his dad, my grandpa Kelly, told him that he should write his name so that people can always understand what it says. He said, "Son, you should be proud of your name. It represents the Kelly family and who you are. When you write your name, make sure it's written so that people know that Jim Kelly signed here." I love my grandpap! My dad listened to his dad. You should see my dad's autograph. It's the best, and you can read it. Let's do this. Come with me to my daddy's office so you can see for yourself how good his autograph is. He's sort of goofy sometimes, so I apologize in advance. Go to:

Cam Clips (CODE: DADDY).

Do you like the way someone else writes? Ask that person to write your full name and their full name right here.

Ask your mother to share **two words** that best describe your personality:

1.

2.

Ask your father to share **two words** that best describe your personality:

1.

2.

If you were to describe your personality, what **three words** would you use?

1.

2.

3.

Lots of people say that character counts! What's that, exactly? My mom says, "Character is who you are when no one but God is looking," and that good character is really important. So good character is doing good things when no one but God can see you, and bad character is sort of seeing what you can get away with when no one is looking.

Cam Jam: We've been talking a lot about *words* in the last few questions. Our words are very important. God has given us words to communicate. Words hold meaning and send a message to the person we're talking to. Sometimes words hurt. I know that a few times I wish I could have taken back the words that came out of my mouth. Unfortunately, I can be sort of sassy to my mom sometimes. My dad says this all the time: "It's not what you say, young lady, it's how you say it." I know when I've said something in a way that I shouldn't because my mom gives me the raised eyebrow look. She doesn't even have to say anything, she just gives me that look and I know. I always feel bad after I've said something that I wish I hadn't. But that's what forgiveness is all about. I'm thankful for the words *I'm sorry*. God surely cares about the words that come out of our mouth. I'm not sure where it says this in the Bible, but God says that the words that come out of our mouth come from our heart. So I guess that means that if I'm not saying very nice things, my heart needs more of God. Don't forget to check out the *SWEET TRUTH*—it's a good one. So let's talk about *words*.

Sweet Truth

Do not let any unwholesome talk come out of your mouths, but only what is helpful for building others up according to their needs, that it may benefit those who listen. (Ephesians 4:49)

Does your mom or dad have that "look," like the one I described that my mom has?

Do you think your words are important?

Do you think God cares about the words that come out of your mouth?

Do you like to encourage your friends and family, to bring out the best in them?

You've been asked to make **two secret message cookies**. What encouraging messages would you put inside them?

1.

2.

Did your words ever make someone cry?

What did you do after you realized that your words hurt someone's feelings?

Has anyone ever hurt your feelings?

What did that person say or do to you?

How did this make you feel?

How did you respond to this person?

Cam Jam: My mom and I have had talks about being hurt by the things people say and do. During our lives we will all experience hurt as a result of someone's words and actions. What matters most is how we respond to that hurt. Sometimes when someone says something to me that hurts, I just want to say something mean right back. But that's never good, and it always makes things worse. I try to pray right away instead of responding. I ask God to help me to forgive that person and move on without trying to throw words back that will hurt him or her. UGH! It's so hard to be nice when someone has hurt you—isn't it? With God's help, there's always a better way.

Sometimes people say mean things because their heart is hurting. You never know what someone might be going through. So as hard as it is, I try to pray for people who are mean.

I have also learned that I should never believe the discouraging words that people say to me. What matters most is what God says about me. His WORDS are really what I should be listening to.

More of what's on the inside...

Do you smile often?

Do you like to make people laugh?

What's the funniest experience you have ever had?

Write down the funniest joke you've ever heard.

Who is the funniest person you know?

Are you quiet and shy or loud and crazy?

Do you like meeting other people?

Leader of the pack or follow the crowd?

Do you stand up for what's right or stay silent?

Bossy or gentle? (Be honest. I admit it; I can be a little bossy sometimes. But I'm a work in progress, and God is helping me to be more and more gentle and gracious.)

Do you go with the flow or get frustrated when things don't go your way?

Would you describe yourself as a last-minute kind of girl or as well prepared?

Are you a people pleaser—always trying to make everyone happy around you?

Are you a problem solver?

Can you keep a secret?

Do you share your feelings with others or keep them to yourself?

Are you sensitive?

Do you care about the needs of others?

Do you like to give gifts?

If you could give anything in the entire world to **two people**, who would you choose and what would you give them?

1.

2.

What **two things** are you most afraid of right now?

1.

2.

What do you do when you're afraid?

Cam Jam: Whenever I'm afraid about something, the first thing I do is tell my mom about it. After I talk to her we usually pray. I love hearing my mom pray. I wish I trusted God all the time, but sometimes I don't. But even when I get scared or worried, God still loves me, and He will help me to trust Him more.

Do you ever pray when you're afraid?

Talk to God about what you're afraid of right now.

What do you do when you're angry?

Are you angry about something right now? What (who)?   Why?

Has anyone ever been mad at you?   Who?

Why was this person mad at you?

What did you do when you found out he or she was mad?

Did you eventually apologize or did you get mad back?

List **three things** that really bug you.

1.

2.

3.

Describe your most embarrassing moment.

What's the coolest thing you've ever done that you'll never forget as long as you live?

What do you spend most of your time doing?

What do you usually do on the weekends?

Favorite free-time activity?

If you could plan an entire day to go the way you want it to, what would you do all day?

Do you like taking risks and trying new things?

Describe a time when you didn't want to try to do something new, but when you finally did it was great—better than you expected.

Do you give up easily or persevere?

Cam Jam: Sometimes I just want to give up. If I'm struggling with homework, a project, or basketball (ugh), I can get so frustrated and discouraged sometimes that I just want to stop and not finish. But that's not good. I need to remind myself (if my mother hasn't already) that God is *for* me. He is always with me and will never leave me. I'm not alone in my struggles, and neither are you. God is our help. What helps me to persevere is knowing and believing that God will help me to press on and not give up.

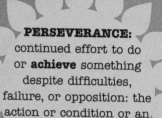

PERSEVERANCE: continued effort to do or **achieve** something despite difficulties, failure, or opposition: the action or condition or an instance of persevering: **steadfastness**.

Sweet Truth

The LORD himself goes before you and will be with you; he will never leave you nor forsake you. Do not be afraid; do not be discouraged. (Deuteronomy 31:8)

Are you a clean freak or kind of sloppy?

Is your room clean right now?

If your room is a mess, go clean it. Your parents will be surprised that you cleaned your room without being asked. Write down what they said after they realized you did this all on your own.

Do you do your best to obey your parents?

Give one example when you chose not to listen to your parents. What happened?

Can you give an example of when it was really hard to obey your parents?

Have you ever been grounded?   Why?

Do you have any habits you wish you could break?   What are they?

Do you ever talk to God when you have a need?

What do you need help with right now?

Cam Jam: I think it's so important to ask for help when you need it. Even though some things might be very personal, it's still very important to find at least one person to talk to whom you trust. God is our help, and He wants us to come to Him first with anything and everything. There's no problem or pain too big for God. He knows exactly what you need at all times. It's not good to keep things bottled up inside. God also gives us people in our lives to help us when we need it.

Here's a prayer journal entry I'd like you to read. It's about asking for help.

> Dear God,
>
> Please help me to not be afraid to ask for help. You are my help, and I can come to You for anything, anytime. Give me the courage to ask for help when I need it. Please give me someone who will help me and guide me during difficult times. Thank You that I do not have to go through anything alone. I have You. Please help me today.

What would you add to this journal entry?

Is it hard for you to tell someone that you're sorry?

If so, why do you think that is?

Do you need to ask someone to forgive you? Who, and for what?

Do you need to forgive someone right now? For what?

Do you need to ask God to forgive you?

Take some time right now to talk to God about this.

Cam Jam: Sometimes I find it hard to forgive someone when they have hurt me. At times I even say to myself, "Why should I forgive her?" When I'm struggling with trying to forgive someone, my mom reminds me of how much God has forgiven me. I'm thankful that no matter what I do or think or say, God forgives me—all the time, every time. If I'm God's chosen girl, I need to be more like Him, and that means I need to forgive like He does—all the time, every time. Ummm, this is easier said than done. I need help to forgive like God does. So where do I get help? I just ask Him for it. Sounds so simple, doesn't it? It is simple if we trust God to help us when we need Him.

Sweet Truth

Bear with each other and forgive whatever grievances you may have against one another. Forgive as the LORD forgave you. (Colossians 3:13)

If you could change one thing about the following, what would it be?

Yourself

Family

Home

Friends

School

World

Describe yourself using one word.

If you could make **three wishes** and knew they would come true, what would they be?

1.

2.

3.

If you could spend an entire day with someone, with whom would you spend your day, and why this person? What would you do with this person all day long?

Whom do you look up to in your life right now?

Write down **two things** about this person that explain why you admire him or her:

1.

2.

Ask this person you look up to or admire to share **two very important life lessons** with you.

1.

2.

What **three life lessons** would you share with a girl younger than you?

1.

2.

3.

Where do you go when you need to be alone?

Where do you go when you need to cry?

Cam Jam: I need to tell you something. It's okay to cry. I cry a lot. In fact, I'm thankful that I get to cry. Can you even imagine what it would be like if we had no tears? How would we express our hearts? Sometimes I cry and I can't stop. Sometimes I have no idea why I'm crying. (My sister cries for no reason at all, but my mom says it's because it's "that time of the month"— whatever.) My dad grew up in a household full of boys, so he wasn't allowed to cry. He didn't get in trouble for crying, but his brothers teased him whenever he cried (and he teased them whenever they cried too)—so all of the boys tried to hide their tears. I'm glad I don't have to hide my tears.

God has a lot to say about tears. You've got to read the *SWEET TRUTH*—it's one of my favorites. It's hard to believe that God puts our tears in a bottle. Nothing is impossible for Him! I'm comforted knowing that He cares enough about me to catch my tears when they fall.

Sweet Truth

You number my wanderings; put my tears in Your bottle; are they not in Your book.

(Psalm 56:8 NKJV)

Finish the sentences:
I love to…

The most amazing day of my life was when...

The worst day of my life was when...

I get most annoyed when...

I can't wait to...

If I could I would...

My heart hurts the most when...

Cam Jam: I miss my brother, Hunter. I'll tell you more about him when we get to the family chapter, but for now all I can say is I miss him. I miss Hunter more than words can describe. I miss everything about him. When I was little I spent every day with my brother. Everything he did, I did—except for the medical stuff he had to do. I can't think about it too much because I'll just cry... I'll cry a lot. So my answer to this question is, My heart hurts the most when I think about my big brother, Hunter.

List **three things** that you think would make you happy if you had them.

1.

2.

3.

List **five things** that you're thankful for.

1.

2.

3.

4.

5.

Do you ever thank God for all that you have?

Write a letter to God for all that you are thankful for right now. Talk to Him about who you are—the wonderful person He created on the inside. Tell Him about what's going on in your heart. Ask Him what He wants your heart to look like. Express how you feel about all that's happening in your life right now. He loves you and He's listening. And best of all, He cares!

The Heart of the Matter
Word Search

```
S  T  A  W  M  I  E  B  I  T  U  X  G  P  E
D  Y  R  U  R  C  C  B  L  V  J  J  U  P  H
R  Y  Z  A  F  X  N  X  S  D  T  R  O  Z  W
O  S  T  E  E  J  E  W  L  Z  I  H  I  F  Z
W  W  E  I  E  H  D  H  D  T  K  W  L  B  L
W  D  Y  W  L  P  I  E  Y  N  M  P  M  U  V
V  C  U  Y  I  A  F  Q  M  K  B  U  F  P  L
L  I  X  S  N  H  N  I  W  O  K  I  S  S  T
T  W  V  Y  G  Q  O  O  Y  M  T  K  J  Y  K
E  R  G  Z  S  K  C  H  S  U  R  I  F  L  G
V  X  F  W  O  C  U  W  A  R  R  V  O  M  M
E  C  N  A  R  E  V  E  S  R  E  P  C  N  A
E  N  I  H  S  T  B  G  Z  T  U  P  W  H  S
C  H  A  R  A  C  T  E  R  P  Z  B  P  N  A
Z  B  P  T  Z  Q  K  W  E  S  K  I  R  V  P
```

BEAUTIFUL	CHARACTER	CONFIDENCE
EMOTIONS	FEELINGS	HEART
HOPE	PERSEVERANCE	PERSONALITY
PURITY	SHINE	WORDS

Sweet Section 4

MY AMAZING FAMILY

Oh my goodness, I love my family so much. My love for them feels like my heart might actually burst. Don't get me wrong; there are some days when I get frustrated with my sister or mad at my mom or dad. But no matter what, I always love them as much as my heart can handle.

I need my family. I can't even imagine life without them. I know that God loves me, because He gave me such a loving and dedicated family. No family is perfect, that's for sure. Every family has its ups and downs, because we all go through hard times. I guess that's one of the blessings of family; they're there for you during difficult times. My mom says that sometimes your family might give you a hard time, but they're only hard on you because they love you. But in the end, they are loyal and loving!

We don't pick our family—God does. He's the one who determined who our mom and dad would be. He knew exactly what He was doing when He selected the family for you and me. I suppose some people have a hard time believing this because they have a bad relationship with their parents or siblings. Just thinking about this makes me want to cry. I hate divorce. Some of my friends are experiencing the pain that comes with a divorce. The two girls I talk about in this book, the ones you've met through **Cam Clips**, Bailey and Kiley, their parents are divorced. My heart hurts for them.

It's really important to remember that whatever your family circumstance is right now, God is always there for you. He will help you and your family to live each and every day for Him. It will all work out, because He promised. And God never breaks His promises. Besides, as His child you are in His family. He is your heavenly Father. He's the best Father. And if He's your Father, He knows exactly what you and your family need right now. He'll take care of you today and always.

Are you ready to talk about your family?

All right! Let's go!

Let's start with the two people who brought you into this world: Your Amazing, Incredible (sometimes annoying), Lovable Parents.

Father's full name:

Mother's full name:

What's your mother's maiden name? (If you don't know what this means, please ask your mom.)

Dad's nickname? (If he doesn't have one now, what was his nickname as a kid?)

Mom's nickname?

Mom's age (GULP)?

Dad's age (tee-hee)?

Ask one of your parents to share the story of how they met each other. Write down some of the details.

What do you think about their story? Is it romantic?

How long have your mom and dad known each other?

How old were your parents when they met?

How old were your parents when you were born?

Time OUT! Do you chew your pencils or pens, Yuk? Just asking...

Okay, time in, back to your parents!

Ask either your mom or dad what **two words** best describe you as a baby.

1.

2.

Ask either of them what **two words** best describe you now.

1.

2.

Have your mom and dad or someone in your family that you trust answer the next six questions. Write both of their answers under each question.

1. What information about boys do I absolutely need to know?

2. What's the most important thing I need to know about God?

3. When life gets really, really hard, what should I do?

4. What should I look for in a best friend?

5. What should I do when I don't know what to do?

6. What's the best advice someone has ever given you? (Who gave you this advice?)

Write down the full names of all of your siblings; include their nicknames, ages, and birthdays:

Are you the oldest, youngest, or somewhere in the middle?

Describe each of your family members using one word.

★⋆ *Cam Fam:* I want to tell you about my brother, Hunter. Wow, I don't even know where to begin. First of all, I should tell you this: My brother went to heaven when he was eight and a half years old. I miss him more than I can possibly explain to you. Hunter was two years older than me. When he was very little, like, just four months old, my parents found out that my brother had a horrible disease. The doctors said that he wouldn't live very long. But God had a different plan, and my brother lived longer than they said he would. I wish I could tell you so many things about Hunter, but my words would fill up at least two books. I guess all you need to know is that he was an amazing and very handsome boy. He never ever spoke a single word and yet he really taught us all so much. The most important thing Hunter taught us is that we need God. Because of Hunter, my entire family (including me) learned to trust God. We all miss him so much, but we know that we will see him again someday in heaven. I can't wait!

Are any of your family members, relatives, or friends sick with a disease such as cancer, or any other type of sickness?

If you said yes to the previous question, write down that person's name.

Is anyone you know (like a family member or friend) disabled?   Who?

Write down **three things** you can do for the person you wrote down above.

1.

2.

3.

Cam Jam: I just thought about this—maybe you don't have any brothers or sisters. I know some kids who are the only child in their family. I can't even imagine what that would be like.

Are you the only child in your family?

If you are an only child, do you ever wish you had a brother or sister?

It's hard for me to ask this question, but I know this might be your circumstance. Are your parents divorced?

Do you ever feel angry or sad about it?

Do you have any stepsisters or stepbrothers? Write down their names and ages.

Cam Jam: This is all very personal stuff, so I better just chill out. I know that a lot of people go through divorce and eventually everything is better. I hope that's the case for you if you live in a divorced family. The best thing to do with all of this is pray. I've prayed for every single girl who reads through this book. So that means I've prayed for you and your circumstances. God has a plan for your life, and He can work all things together for good!

Create an acrostic poem that describes your family.

F —
A —
M —
I —
L —
Y —

Certainly, pets are an important part of the family.

Do you have any pets?   If you do, what pets do you have and what are their names?

 Cam Fam: I have three dogs, which I will introduce to you. Two of them are Labrador retrievers, or Labs for short, and the other one is a Chihuahua. They're so cute. I can't wait for you to meet them. You're going to love them just as much as I do—at least I think you will. All three of them are so different and absolutely adorable. I have so much to tell you about Butterscotch, Buddy, and Bella, but I'll talk to you in person. Come on, let's go watch:

Cam Clips (CODE: DOGS).

What tricks can your pet(s) do?

Did you ever make your babysitter do a pet trick? (LOL)

Do you sleep with any of your pets?

⭐ *Cam Fam:* Please don't tell me that you sleep with your pet guinea pig and turtle. That wouldn't be right. I suppose it would be much worse if you slept with your pet spider. No way! I can't even picture it. Our Chichi, Bella, sleeps with my mom and dad. She drives my dad crazy. During the night, Bella gets up to go to the bathroom at least three times. Before she hops off the bed she always shakes her body and that really aggravates my dad. The worst is when Bella forgets to pee and poop on her puppy pad. Oh dear, you don't want to be around when my dad steps on Bella's poop in the middle of the night. It's a good thing I sleep in a different room.

Favorite type of dog?

I ask a lot about dogs because I'm a dog lover. You might be a cat lover instead. What is your favorite type of cat?

Top **two favorite** pet names?

1.

2.

Did you ever own a goldfish or two or three?

What did you name your fish?

Mom and Dad just told you that you can have as many animals as you want. (Can you even imagine?) What animals would you choose to have as family pets, and what would you name them?

Let's talk about your home.

Describe what your house looks like...color and stuff like that.

How long have you lived in the house you live in right now?

How many times have you moved?

How many floors in your house?

What's your favorite room in the house?

How many TVs do you have?

Do you have a computer?

Do you have a fireplace?   (If you have one, do your parents make fires in your fireplace?)

How many bathrooms do you have?

Do you have your own bathroom?

Is your bedroom on the first or second floor?

Do you share a room with one of your siblings?

Erin: Well, I would have my own room, but Cam has to sleep with me. Right, Camryn? I don't really mind, but sometimes I wish I could have my room all to myself.

★ *Cam Fam:* Yes, it's true. Even though Erin and I have our own rooms, I sleep in her room every night. I don't know, I guess I feel safer with my sissy. Besides, we've always been together. Even when Hunter was here, we were always together. At least we don't have to share the same closet and bathroom. That would be tough. I need my mirror space. Right, Erin?!

Your bedroom is a special place. Mom and Dad have decided that it's time to redecorate. What would you do to your bedroom if you could do anything you wanted to do?

I can't leave home without it! List **three things** you never leave home without.

1.

2.

3.

How do you and your family start each day?

What is the typical morning routine at your house?

★☆ *Cam Fam:* We have a morning routine. Usually, my mom comes into the bedroom first. She plops Bella down on the bed and then snuggles in between Erin and me. If she turns on a light, it's always dim, because Erin and I can't deal with bright lights early in the morning. Before we roll out of bed to get ready, my mom always prays. I'm usually still half asleep when my mom is praying, but I always hear the ending of her prayers because she ends her morning prayer the same every single day. This is what she prays:

> *We put on the full armor of God today. We put on the helmet of salvation to protect our*

minds because we have the mind of Christ. We put on the breastplate of righteousness; to protect our hearts...create in us a pure heart, Lord. Belt of truth; we will not listen to any lies from the enemy nor tell any lies. We will listen to the Voice of truth. Boots fitted with the Gospel of peace; wherever we go, please help us to bring the Good News. Shield of Faith, which extinguishes all the fiery darts from the enemy. And the sword of the Spirit, which is the Word of God. Please hide Your Word in our hearts so that we will not sin against You.

While my mom is saying this prayer, we have body motions that go with it. We're usually too tired to do them, but my mom still does them. Sometimes she'll move my arms for me to put on my helmet and boots. Not a real helmet and pair of boots, of course. It's as though we're getting dressed in our God armor for the day. We're preparing ourselves for the day ahead of us.

After my mom finishes praying, we get up and get dressed for school. (In the summer, we sleep in—I LOVE sleeping in, even though I don't sleep half the day away like my sissy does.) My parents work together to get breakfast and our school lunches ready. My dad always puts ESPN on in the kitchen every morning. And it's always so loud (I think my dad is losing his hearing. I know one of his ears is not good from all the football he played. I think the good ear is going now too. Sheesh!) This drives my mom crazy. She likes it calm and quiet in the morning. I don't think any of my family members are morning people. Erin for sure isn't a morning girl. Yikes! I won't even go there.

The last morning routine thing for the Kelly crew is the kiss good-bye. We always kiss good-bye, even if we're in a hurry. Also, before I walk into school, I ask my mom every single day to pray for me and she responds every time by saying, "Always, Camryn, you know it." Knowing that my mom is praying for me while I'm at school means a lot to me.

What is your bedtime routine?

Cam Fam: We have a bedtime routine but it changes sometimes depending on what's going on. Most of the time it looks something like this: Before we go to bed, Erin and I have to have our school outfits all picked out and our backpacks by the back door. I also have to have my lunch snacks packed up and ready to go. We try to get as much done as possible the night before, so that we're not scurrying around in the morning (and so my dad isn't constantly telling us to hurry up).

Once we have our face washed and teeth brushed and we're snuggled into bed, we pray. If my dad's home, we all pray together. My daddy kneels at the end of our bed and Mommy snuggles up between Erin and me. Usually my dad prays first, but not always. His prayers are not long at all. But then my mom prays. Sometimes she prays so long that my sister and I (*and even my daddy sometimes*) fall asleep while she's praying. That's why we usually have her pray last. If we're still awake, my mother will say this to Erin and me before we turn the light off:

> *May the Lord bless and keep you. May He make His face shine down upon you and bring you peace. May you know the love God has for you. May you know that perfect love casts out all fear. May the Lord bless you with wisdom and revelation, so you can know Him better. May you be pure in heart, mind, and body. May you be strong and courageous. May you know how much God loves you and how much Mommy and Daddy love you too. In Jesus' name...Amen.*

I love when my family prays. I just know that no matter what happens I can always count on my mom and dad to pray for me.

When do you usually pray...before you go to bed, before you eat?

Do you pray with your family?

Who usually prays in your family?

Would you rather pray with someone or by yourself?

Are you comfortable praying out loud in front of people?

Have you ever asked anyone to pray for you?

What was going on in your life that you needed prayer?

Do you believe God hears you when you pray?

Cam Jam: God hears you! I know this because He says He knows the words on your tongue before you even speak them. Check out the *SWEET TRUTH*.

Sweet Truth

Before a word is on my tongue you know it completely, O Lord.

(Psalm 139:4)

Have you ever fallen asleep while someone else is praying?

Have you ever fallen asleep while *you* were praying?

Have you ever burst out laughing while someone else was praying?

Cam Jam: I've done this and I felt so bad. The person praying didn't care at all. Thank God. I wasn't laughing at the person. I laughed at what was said because it was funny. Besides, God loves when we laugh. He gave us the gift of laughter. However, I suppose laughing during prayer isn't such a good idea. But it's a good thing God knows my heart, and He loves me anyway.

Since we've been talking a lot about prayer, would it be okay for me to pray for you?

I hope you said yes. (Please write your name in the blanks.)

> Dear God,
> Thank You for Hot Chocolate with God and for the girl holding this book right now. You know every need my friend _____ has right now. You love _____ more than I can even imagine. Lord, I pray that you will help _____ to know how much You love her. Help her to know

that she is never alone. Show her how great You really are. Help _____ to trust You at all times. When her heart is broken, please help her to turn to You for comfort. When _____ is afraid, please give her courage and help her to know that You will protect her from all harm. If _____ is confused, please help her to get the help that she needs because You are not a God of confusion. If _____ doesn't know who You are, would You please show her Yourself? God, You are amazing. You are awesome! Please bless my friend _____ today! Thank You so much!

Thank you for letting me pray for you. I think I'm taking after my mom because I could have gone on and on. You don't really ever have to stop praying. Praying is just talking to God. I think He would love it if we talked to Him about everything, all the time. In fact, I should pray more for sure.

Let's talk some more about your Amazing Family...

Eight Random Family Questions

1. Does your family have an American flag?

2. Who carves the Thanksgiving turkey?

3. Who's the funniest family member?

4. Relative with the weirdest hair?

5. Who gives the best bear hugs?

6. Relative who's most likely to fall asleep in the middle of a party?

7. Did you ever have a mouse in your house?

8. If you could add someone to your family, who would it be, and why?

⭐ *Cam Fam:* I would like to add Justin Bieber to my family, for obvious reasons. Oh brother, I crack myself up. I would also add my besties, Bailey and Kiley, to my family, but they're like family already.

Do both of your parents work?

What do your parents do?

Family car(s)—what do your parents drive you around in?

Which family member do you feel most comfortable talking to?

Who takes care of you when you get sick?

When you need help, whom do you go to?

Favorite home-cooked meal?

By the way, is your mother a good cook?

⭐ *Cam Fam:* I won't tell her if you say no! My mom is still trying to learn how to cook. She makes a very tasty meat loaf and a delicious brown sugar chicken dish thing. But my dad is the better cook, and my mom knows it. Even if my mom cooks something that I think is totally gross, I don't want her to feel bad so I at least try it… Sometimes.

What do you know how to cook? (Hmmmmm, could you maybe teach my mom that recipe??? PLEASE!!!!!!!!!!!!!!!!!!!) (Just told you, I crack myself up!)

Family holiday traditions (Whom do you spend the holidays with? Where do you go on certain holidays?)

Who usually cooks Thanksgiving dinner in your house?

What's your favorite part of Thanksgiving dinner?

If it was up to you, what would you serve on Thanksgiving?

Whom do you spend Christmas with?

Can you tell me what you think the real meaning of Christmas is?

★★ *Cam Fam:* We believe that Christmas is the birth of Jesus, God's one and only Son. We celebrate His birth because if He hadn't come to Earth we would have no hope and we would have no eternity in heaven. Every year before we open our presents we give a gift to Jesus. It's His birthday! After we pray and thank God for all the many blessings He has given us—especially His Son—we write our names on little paper hearts. Our gift to Jesus is our heart. We each have a little paper heart and we put our name on the front and the date on the back. After we're done we put our hearts in a small trinket box until next year. I love doing this as a family. It's a reminder for us that Christmas is His birthday. He is the greatest gift of all! And the greatest gift we can give Him is the gift of our heart, I mean to love Him and serve Him from our heart. I can't wait for Christmas!

Do you send out a family picture with your Christmas card every year?

Do you have a fake or real tree for Christmas?

What's your favorite Christmas movie?

 Cam Fam: I love the movie *Elf*. Just thinking about this movie cracks me up. It's my dad's favorite movie too.

Dream Christmas list: What **four gifts** would you love to receive for Christmas?

1.

2.

3.

4.

If you could give Jesus a gift for His birthday, what would you give HIM?

Maybe you don't celebrate Christmas. List all the other holidays you celebrate.

Let's talk a little bit about aunts and uncles and the rest of your extended family...

Would you say that you come from a big family?

What are your dad's mom's and dad's names (your grandparents on your dad's side)?

What are your mom's mom's and dad's names (your grandparents on your mom's side)?

Are all four of your grandparents still alive?

Do you live near your grandparents?

How often do you get to see your grandma and grandpa (from both sides)?

Does your grandma ever pinch your cheeks?

How many aunts and uncles do you have on both sides of your family?

Write down the names of all your mom's siblings. Next to your mom's brothers' and sisters' names (your aunts and uncles), write down the names of all their kids (otherwise known as your first cousins). You might not need all the space that's been provided…But then again, you might even need more space.

Now write down the names of all your dad's siblings. Next to your dad's brothers' and sisters' names (your aunts and uncles), write down the names of all their kids. (Does your hand hurt from writing so much? This is all great stuff to know and share, so it's worth it to write it all down.)

On both sides of your family, who is the oldest and youngest person? Write their ages and names here. (You might have to ask your parents.)

Where do some of your relatives live? List the states and who lives there.

Do you have any cousins who are the same age as you right now?   Who?

Who's your favorite aunt?
Why?

Who's your favorite uncle?
Why?

Who's your favorite cousin on your mom's side of the family?   Why?

Who's your favorite cousin on your dad's side of the family?   Why?

Which relatives do you spend the most time with?

What do you usually do with these relatives?

What about church?

Do you and your family attend church?

If you do, what's the name of your church?

Do you go to a big church or a small one?

Do you attend the adult service or do you go to the kids' session?

Do you usually sit in the same place every Sunday?

Are your pastor's sermons interesting or zzzzzzzzzzzzzzz?

What's the music like?

Do you like going to church? (Be honest!)

Cam Jam: I'm sorry to say this, but sometimes I really don't want to go to church. I don't like when I feel that way, but it's the truth. It's not that I don't like church; it's just that I'd like to sleep in longer. Our church is, like, thirty minutes away and it's always packed with lots of people so we have to leave extra early. When we go to church, I love it. It's great that my grandpa and grandma and many of my other relatives go to our church. We all usually sit together in the back right corner. It's, like, our spot. My favorite thing about our church is listening to our pastor. I think God speaks through him. Oh, and I love the music—it's so beautiful. Sometimes during the worship (or singing time) my mom cries. I don't like when my mom cries, but it's not a sad cry, it's a happy, thankful cry. At least that's what she calls it. Either way, when my mom cries, I want to cry too. And I guess if we're both going to cry then church is a good place to do it.

If you don't go to church, do you wish you did?

Finish the sentences below.

My greatest fear that concerns my family is . . .

I wish my family . . .

The most unusual thing about my family is . . .

The thing I love best about my family is . . .

My Amazing Family Word Search

```
L  D  T  O  N  Y  D  A  D  E  N  N  Y  C  R
O  L  Z  E  L  W  U  D  I  X  R  T  P  E  L
V  J  Z  I  G  N  A  Q  V  J  E  A  L  K  I
E  U  M  H  Y  U  K  W  N  N  H  A  A  O  V
K  A  Z  B  I  S  J  H  Z  I  T  G  C  L  X
F  A  L  Q  S  W  G  M  X  I  E  Z  A  M  T
H  O  M  E  X  C  I  N  V  N  G  B  F  P  R
D  O  E  A  S  L  P  E  I  A  O  I  I  F  A
M  U  P  Z  Y  S  S  L  P  L  T  R  P  Y  D
Q  N  E  R  D  L  I  H  C  E  B  T  P  J  I
N  Z  I  A  X  Y  Q  Y  X  V  T  I  J  U  T
O  O  K  E  E  X  Z  W  H  E  W  S  S  R  I
R  Y  S  I  E  S  F  Z  V  A  V  A  M  C  O
Q  A  O  Y  P  P  N  X  O  J  K  A  B  Q  N
R  J  X  J  R  A  B  W  C  F  D  V  W  A  S
```

CHILDREN	DAD	FAMILY
HOME	JOY	LOVE
MOM	PETS	RELATIVES
SIBLINGS	TOGETHER	TRADITIONS

120

Sweet Section 5

Friends, School, and Whatever...

Other than your family, your friends are some of the most important people in your life. My dad says this all the time: "You are who you hang out with." I think what my dad is trying to say is that your friends have a huge influence in your life—so choose them wisely. We can't choose our family members but we *can* choose whom we decide to be friends with. I hope your friendship experience has been a great one so far. We all go through rough times with our friends, that's for sure. We are all learning as we grow. Learning how to be a good friend is one of the most important things we can learn as a tween girl. It's important to *be* a good friend so that you can have great friendships. In fact, a great friendship must start with you first. I've certainly had my ups and downs as far as friends are concerned. But you know what? God always ends up showing me my heart in the situation. Whenever I had an issue, I was the one that God wanted to teach. I really do want to be a true and faithful friend, don't you? I know I need God's help to be the best friend I can possibly be.

So let's talk about friendships and school and all the other fun stuff life as a tween girl is made up of. You spend a lot of time in school, so I'm sure you have a lot to share about your experiences there. I'm not a huge school fan right now. Don't get me wrong, I know that school is important and that we all need to learn, it's just that I wish we didn't have to spend so much time there. Do you know what I mean? I was thinking that maybe school should be just three days a week. I also think that we should start the school day much later, like maybe ten in the morning instead of when it's still dark—sheesh. Yeah, I have a lot of ideas. Regardless, I know school can be great if my attitude is great. *Oh Lord, please change my attitude about school.* Yeah, I pray a lot about school and friendships. I can't wait to hear what you have to say!

Where do you go to school?

Where is your school located?

Do you take a bus, walk, or get a ride to school? How long does it take you to get there?

Cam Jam: The school I go to is about thirty minutes away (unless there's a lot of traffic) from my house. I don't take a bus, so every day either my mom or dad drives my sister and me. The drive to school is the worst. You would not believe the traffic. We're late a lot and of course that's not good, but we do the best that we can.

Right now I'm in sixth grade and my sissy is in tenth

grade. By the time you read this we'll both be in the next grade level. My three cousins go to our school too. It's great knowing that my family is there, especially on days when school is not going so well. I struggle in school with Social Studies. I don't know why, but my Social Studies tests are so confusing.

I have to wear a uniform every day. I've decided to show you my uniform rather than try to explain what it looks like. Check it out online at:

ᵁ Cam Clips (CODE: UNIFORM).

Do you attend a private or public school?

Is your school big or small?

Does your school start with kindergarten and go all the way to twelfth grade? _____ If not, what grade does your school go up to?

What grade are you in right now?

Do you have a school ID with your picture on it?

What time do you wake up and go to bed on school days?

What time do you start and end school?

Do you have homeroom?

Who is your homeroom teacher?

Who do you usually sit next to in homeroom?

Do you say the Pledge of Allegiance in the morning before classes start?

How many kids are in your class?   (Because my school is so small, this is an easy question. But if you go to a really big school you might have to ask someone to find out the answer to this.)

How many teachers do you have?

Do you switch teachers every period?

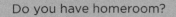

Who is your favorite teacher and why?

If you could have a celebrity teacher, who would it be, and why this person?

Do you have a locker?

Who has the lockers to the left and right of you?

Do you carry a backpack?

What's in your backpack right now? Describe what your backpack looks like. Write everything down.

Cam Jam: My dad thinks I have way too many backpacks and purses. He doesn't think I need a new backpack for school every year. And he so doesn't get the fact that a girl can never have too many purses. I'm not sure if he understands what my backpacks go through each and every day during the school year. They get beat up pretty bad. Drinks and snacks get spilled all over the inside. My backpack for school this year already got ruined because one of the straps completely ripped off. Whatever. My mom loves bags so it's easier to talk to her about my purse and bag needs.

Are you allowed to chew gum in school?

Are you allowed to have cell phones in school?

Do you have to wear a uniform?

If you wear a uniform, describe what it looks like.

How many periods do you have during the typical school day?

What's your school schedule for each day of the week?

Monday:

Tuesday:

Wednesday:

Thursday:

Friday:

What are your favorite and least favorite subjects?

Do you get letter or number grades?

Have you ever been on the Honor or Merit Roll?

What was your best overall average for a semester or quarter?

Best grade and worst grade you've ever received, and in what subjects?

Do you have to take midterms yet? (Not fun—not fun at all.)

 What foreign language are you learning?

What book are you reading right now for English?

What are you learning about right now in Science?

What are you learning about right now in Social Studies? (UGH!)

Do you like doing school projects?

Do you enjoy working with other students in a group or working alone?

Do you raise your hand and ask questions in class? If not, why?

Do you like PE or gym class?

What's your favorite PE activity?

Do you have to take a fitness test in gym?

Cam Jam: I'm not big on bragging about myself, but I just have to tell you this. We had our fitness test not too long ago and I had to do the long jump. Okay, take a deep breath because you're not going to believe how far I jumped. I jumped 6' 3"—that's six feet, three inches. Isn't that crazy? My parents were shocked and very proud of me. I think my gym teacher was shocked too. Maybe I should consider being on the track team. HMMMM...

Does your school have an indoor swimming pool?

What school sports do you have?

What school sports do you play?

What's your school mascot? (We are the Crusaders.)

Lunchtime...yippee! How much time do you get for lunch?

Favorite school lunch?

How much does your school lunch cost?

What's your absolute favorite lunch from home?

Cam Jam: Please tell me your favorite is a peanut butter sandwich with the crust cut off! If that's your kind of sandwich, you're a girl after my own heart! Oh, and the more snacks I can pack in my lunch bag the better.

Speaking of lunch bags, we've got some cute ones.
Who do you usually sit next to at lunch?

How long is the longest you've been out of school?
(Like, if you were sick or went away with family.)

Have you ever spent any time in the nurse's office?
What happened?

Did you ever get sent to the principal's office?
For what?

Have you ever had to serve a detention?   Why?

Top **three favorite things** about your school:

1.

2.

3.

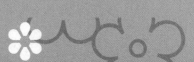

Three changes you would make at your school:

1.

2.

3.

Imagine for a minute that you're the new girl in school. What would you do to try to get to know your new school and meet friends?
Would you be nervous?

When a new girl comes to your school, what do you do? Do you introduce yourself?

What do you do when you see that a classmate has no one to sit with at lunch?

Do you stick up for your friends when they are being teased or bullied?

Have you ever been bullied?　　　Explain what happened.
Describe how it made you feel.

Friends Rock...

Who was your very first friend ever?

Is the person you named in the previous question still your friend?   If not, why?

How old were you when you met your first friend?

BFF...Best Friends Forever

Who is your very best friend?

Describe what your bestie looks like.

When and where did you meet your best friend?

How far away from your house does your BFF live?

Does she or he (hmmm yeah, I just thought about this—your best friend might be a boy rather than a girl) go to the same school that you do?

Do you play on any sports teams together?

Do you and your bestie have sleepovers?

Cam Jam: I'm not big on sleepovers. Wait, I should make myself clear on this—I like having sleepovers at my house, but I don't really like sleeping over at other people's houses. I'm still not very comfortable staying over at a friend's house. And my mom says that's okay. I'm sure I'll be ready by the time I'm older, like in my late teen years or whatever. I NEED my own bed, and that's all there is to it. I guess I need to know my mom is nearby too. Yeah, I admit it; I'm still a Mommy's girl.

Whose house do you usually sleep over at?

Imagine having a twenty-four-hour BFF Day. What **three cool things** would you do?

Where would you go? (Feel free to consult your BFF for this one.)

1.

2.

3.

Create an acrostic poem describing all the qualities that you would hope for in a Best Friend.

B –

E –

S –

T –

F –

R –

I –

E –

N –

D –

Do you have a secret or special handshake with your best bud?

Cam Jam: I do. In fact, I have lots of cool handshakes to show you. You can see them at www .hotchocolatewithgod.com,

Cam Clips (CODE: HANDSHAKE).

What do you and your best friend have in common?

Describe the best time you've ever had with your BFF.

Do you *love* your best friend?

Cam Jam: Love is a very strong word and emotion. People say they love hamburgers and then they turn around and say they love people. That's weird. Certainly, you can't love a hamburger and a person in the same way. I don't see how you can love a hamburger at all. Gross! A friend is supposed to love at all times. This is very hard. Read the *SWEET TRUTH*. Without God's help we don't know how to love. God says in His Word that He *is* love. In order for us to truly love anyone, we need God's love in our hearts first. Do you have God's love *in* your heart? Do you want God's love *in* your heart? We'll talk more about this at the end of this cool, amazing, fun book. Okay?

A friend loves at all times.
(Proverbs 17:17)

You'll need to get together with your BFF for the next few questions. She or he will need to fill out this section. And then when your friend is done answering these questions you need to answer them too. Both of you should write your answers here. Got that?!

YOUR BEST FRIEND MUST ANSWER THE NEXT SEVEN QUESTIONS. (I hope I made myself clear. ☺)

1. What do you love most about me?

2. What **two things** do you like to do with me when we're together?

    1.

    2.

3. What **one** word best describes me?

4. Can you trust me with your biggest secrets?

5. What do you think our best memory together is?

6. How do you think we can make our friendship even better?

7. What do you wish we could do together that we haven't done?

Now that you're together, I have a really special thing that I think you should do right now. Why don't you pray together? Maybe you've never done this before and feel kind of weird about it. I'll make it easy for you. I'll write a prayer for you. All you two have to do is decide who is going to read the prayer out loud. You should be praying for each other. We all need prayer.

Dear God,

Thank you for the gift of friendship. We are so blessed to be best friends. Help us to love each other more and more as our friendship grows. Help us to love You more too. Lord, we need Your help to always be kind and loving. Please teach us how to be the best kind of friend we possibly can be. Help us to be patient and understanding. Help us to not hold a grudge and to always forgive. Lord, fill our hearts with all that is pure, lovely, honest, and good. Thank You that we can come to You at all times. Please, Lord, help us to trust You with our friendship and know that You love us more than we can imagine. Amen.

So how did it go?

What **three things** do you think you can do to *be* a better friend?

1.

2.

3.

Number these friend qualities in the order of their importance to you (give the number 1 to the most important quality and go from there).

_____ **Honesty**—She would never lie to me.

_____ **Sense of humor**—I always laugh whenever we're together.

_____ **Loving**—I feel loved for real by her.

_____ **Forgiving**—When I make a mistake, she is quick to forgive.

_____ **Dependable**—She's always there for me.

_____ **Patient**—She understands me and is never pushy.

_____ **Encouraging**—She lifts me up when I am down.

_____ **Giving**—She would give me her last dollar if I needed it.

_____ **Sincere**—She really cares about me.

_____ **Faith**—I see Jesus in her. She is a girl of faith.

_____ **Selfless**—She always puts others before herself.

Okay, now go back to this list and put your BFF's initials next to the qualities that you see in her. You're not done yet! Go back to the above list and write your initials next to the qualities that you believe you possess as a friend. Wait, one more thing. Of all the friendship qualities listed above, where can you improve?

If you could have a celebrity BFF, who would it be?

Three things that your friends don't know about you:

1.

2.

3.

What do you do when your friend is sad?

What **two things** can you do for your friend when she is sad?

1.

2.

Take some time right now to write a letter or card of encouragement to your hurting friend.

Write down what your friend said after receiving the letter or card you gave her or him.

True Friend Word Search

```
E A Z V M P A W D J L C M S L
C H G D C O J N Z U A Q B I A
Z A N F H E I N F R U W Y N Y
Z F I H U K T H I H K U N C O
U A G U Z N T N G E W R M E L
M M A G U I G P G N W G O R S
O C R Q A T R U S T I N G E B
L F U F P E S M Z G S V N L V
O F O N Z A C X Y S B V O Y K
N I C E C N T L I F T M O L B
A S N Y U I N I O D C A C Q H
K Y E C B U B L E H U K Q N Z
K A H C Z V N S L N W F D W T
L O T U K M T X D G T S E Z C
T S E N O H G V S C Y Q O T O
```

CARING	ENCOURAGING	FAITHFUL
FUN	HONEST	KIND
LOVING	LOYAL	NICE
PATIENT	SINCERE	TRUSTING

Sweet Section 6

Hopes, Dreams, and What My Heart Longs For

What does your heart long for? What do you hope for? God created you and me with the ability to imagine and dream. He gave us the gift of life and the desire for things beyond this life. God blessed us with hope so that no matter what our circumstances are we can always press on with courage. God is at work in our lives at all times, and it's fun to imagine what He might be up to. Do you ever wonder what life will be like in the future—like ten or twenty years from now? Do you sometimes daydream about your life and how it will all turn out? That's what this chapter is about. It's about letting your mind and heart discover what you long for. It's about using your imagination. It's about being the creative young lady God made you to be. We all have dreams of what life could be like. So here's your chance to express your hopes and dreams—and what your heart really longs for.

First, let's talk about some real dreams you've had.

Best dream ever:

Worst dream ever:

Weirdest dream ever:

If you could pack up your suitcase and go away on a dream vacation to anywhere in the world right now, where would you go, and why did you pick this destination?

What do you hope to do for the rest of your life?

Cam Jam: Whoa, now that's a big, crazy question. Don't worry, if you don't really know what you want to do with the rest of your life, that's okay. It's fun to imagine and dream about what life will be like though. God already knows what He has planned for you, so follow Him and He will lead you where you need to be at all times. And remember, it's one day at a time. Oh, and as my mom always says, "One day at a time…one prayer at a time…all in His perfect time."

Do you plan to go to college after you graduate from high school?

What would you like to study in college?

Cam Jam: I've never thought about college, but my sister, Erin, has. Just thinking about my sister not being here makes me really sad. She's four years older than me, so when I'm heading into high school, she'll be going to college. UGH! What am I going to do? I sure hope she doesn't go away to school. Who will I share a room with? Who will I talk to? Yes, my mom is always there for me whenever I need her, but she's not my sissy. Talking about college reminds me that we're all getting older. Okay, enough then, no more college stuff. Besides, I'm not even a teenager yet.

Ask any one of your family members to share **three things** that they imagine for your future.

1.

2.

 3.

Do you hope to get married someday?

It's weird talking about being married, isn't it? Go and grab either your mom or dad and ask them to tell you what **four things** they hope for in a husband and family for you.

1.

2.

3.

4.

Would you like to have a family someday?

How many children would you like to have?

What would you like to name your children?

If God were to sit down and ask you what you would like to do as you live the rest of your days on this earth, what would you tell Him?

List **three questions** you would ask God if He was sitting right next to you right now:

1.

2.

3.

Do you believe in heaven?

Describe what you think heaven looks like?

Who do you know that's in heaven right now?

How do you remember special people who are gone?

Cam Jam: I'll never, ever forget my brother, Hunter, so I don't really need anything to help me to remember him. But I do have some special things that my grammie made for me as special Hunter reminders. After my brother went to heaven, my grammie decided to make all of us beautiful, soft quilts with all the sheets that Hunter used while he was here. Hunter always had the softest sheets and pillowcases. I sleep with my Hunter blanket every single night. If we go out of town, I always bring my Hunter blanket with me. My mom and Erin always bring their special blankets too. Ya know what, I'm going to show you my blanket and some other special things. Check out this:

Cam Clips (CODE: SPECIAL).

What **five things** would you like to do before you go to heaven?

1.

2.

3.

4.

5.

Imagine what it would be like if all of your hopes and dreams came true. Fill in the bubbles with all that you are hoping for right now.

One hundred years from now, what do you think the world will be like? Will people still drive cars? What do you think cell phones will look like? And so forth.

What do you hope your life will be like in fifteen years?

What talent do you wish you had?

If you had a treasure box and could put only **four special things** in it that would be with you forever, what would you put in your box?

1.

2.

3.

4.

Finish these sentences...

My heart's desire is...

I hope that...

Saying Good-bye

Just a few more fun things before you go. I don't want to say good-bye. I've had so much fun, and I don't want it to end. I hope you feel the same way.

Did you pick this book out or did someone give it to you? If it was a gift to you, who gave you *Hot Chocolate with God*—the best book in the universe (after the Bible, of course)?

What **three spectacular ideas** would you add to this book series if you could?

1.

2.

3.

Now send these ideas to us at
www.hotchocolatewithgod.com.

Design It: We've decided to have you design our next *Hot Chocolate with God* book cover.

If you could get some more *Hot Chocolate with God* books to give to friends and family, whom would you give them to? Make a list.

So here are a few questions before we wrap it up:
Where do you think you'll be in five years?
Maybe coming near the end of your teen years?

Where do you think you'll be in ten years?
Maybe graduating college?

How about in fifteen years?
"Here comes the bride, here comes the bride?"

What about twenty-five years?
A busy mom with three or four children—maybe even tweens! GULP!

Okay, that's all normal, you're doing great...

Where will you be in fifty years?
Maybe a gramma?

Now it gets interesting, where will you be in a hundred years?
You could live that long; think about it. But if I ask where will you be in two hundred years...Well, I'm hoping with me and Jesus.

You should know me by now, girlfriend. I can't say good-bye without praying for you one more time. So here we go, and don't forget to write your name in the spaces...

Heavenly Father,
Thank you for the time you've allowed _____ and me to spend together. We've talked and laughed a lot and maybe even cried together too. All of this is a gift from You. Thank You for _____. When she forgets, please remind her of how much You love her. _____ is beautiful. Help her to know that she is a beautiful young tween princess of the King. I pray that every time she looks into the mirror, You will remind her that she is special and unique. Whisper in her ear and write this on her heart: "_____, there's no one like you in the entire world. You are beautiful and wonderful, just the way I made you." Help her to look to You and know that she is loved. When _____ is sad or upset, please help her to know that You've got her

and that You know what's best. Help her to be strong and courageous. Help her set her mind on whatever is true and pure. Teach her how to be a blessing and encouragement to all of the people in her life—especially her family and friends. Lord, You know that I could go on and on. Lastly, please help _____ to give her whole heart and life to You because You are good and loving...and because You love her more than she can even imagine. Thank You for taking care of my new friend!

So I guess this is good-bye. I'm not very good at saying good-bye, so let's just say until next time. Hopefully, I will see you again...in the pages of our next book or maybe on the website. No matter what, let's stay in touch. Okay?

I almost forgot—sheesh, come on, Cam. Here's one more *SWEET TRUTH* for the road. And it's one of my favorites.

Sweet Truth

"For I know the plans I have for you," declares the LORD, "plans to prosper you and not to harm you, plans to give you hope and a future. Then you will call upon me

and come and pray to me, and I will listen to you. You will seek me and find me when you seek me with all your heart." (Jeremiah 29:11–13)

You go, girl!

Shine on!

P.S. You're beautiful!!

P.P.S. God loves you!

P.P.P.S. One more thing…I hope you think of me the next time you're enjoying a nice yummy cup of hot chocolate. Love ya!

Puzzle Solutions

Camryn's Favorite Things Word Search Solution

```
+ + + + + + + + + + + + E + S
E T A L O C O H C T O H C + E
R + + + Y + + + + + + N + I
+ E + + + D + + + + + A + R
+ J G B L A N K E T S + D + R
+ + O N + T + A + + P + + + E
+ + + U I + + + C A U + + + B
+ + + G R F + + U + R + + + P
+ + E + + N R H + + P + + + S
+ R + + + + A E + + L + + + A
S + + + + U + L T + E S + + R
+ + + + H + + + S T N + + + +
+ + + I + + + + + E U + + + +
+ + H + + + + + P + + B + + . +
+ C E L B I B + + + + + + + +
```

(Over, Down, Direction)
BIBLE (7,15,W) BLANKETS (4,5,E)
BUTTERFINGER (12,14,NW) CANDY (9,7,NW)
CHIHUAHUA (2,15,NE) DANCE (13,5,N)
HOT CHOCOLATE (12,2,W) JOURNALS (2,5,SE)
PENS (9,14,NE) PURPLE (11,6,S)
RASPBERRIES (15,11,N) TIGERS (6,6,SW)

This Is Me...This Is My Life Double Puzzle Solution

Unique

Special

Wonderful

Faith

Purity

Loved

Purpose

Life

Answer: You Are Beautiful

Body and Beauty Word Search Solution

```
+ + + L + + M + + + + + + + +
+ + + + U I + + G + + + + + +
+ + + + R F + N Y + + + L E +
+ + + R + + I + + T + + U G C
+ + O + + G + T + + U + F A L
+ R + + N + + + U + + A R M O
E C N A R A E P P A + + E I T
+ + H + G + + + + + E + D B H
+ C + + + R + + + + + B N + E
E U Q I N U O + + + + + O + S
F A S H I O N W Y + + + W + +
+ + + + + + D I + + + + + + +
+ + + + + + O + + N + + + + +
+ + + + + B + + + G + + + + +
+ + + + + + + + + + + + + + +
```

(Over, Down, Direction)

APPEARANCE (10,7,W) BEAUTIFUL (12,9,NW)

BEAUTY (14,8,NW) BODY (6,14,NE)

CHANGING (2,9,NE) CLOTHES (15,4,S)

FASHION (1,11,E) GROWING (5,8,SE)

IMAGE (14,7,N) MIRROR (7,1,SW)

UNIQUE (6,10,W) WONDERFUL (13,11,N)

The Heart of the Matter Word Search Solution

```
S T + + + + E + + + + + + P E
D + R + + + C + + + + + U P +
R Y + A F + N + + + + R O + +
O + T + E + E + + + I H + + +
W + + I E H D + + T + + + + L
+ + + + L + I E Y + + + + U +
+ + + + I A F + M + + + F + +
+ + + + N + N + + O + I + + +
+ + + + G + O O + + T + + + +
+ + + + S + C + S U + I + + +
+ + + + + + + + A R + + O + +
E C N A R E V E S R E P + N +
E N I H S + B + + + + P + + S
C H A R A C T E R + + + + + +
+ + + + + + + + + + + + + + +
```

(Over, Down, Direction)
BEAUTIFUL (7,13,NE) CHARACTER (1,14,E)
CONFIDENCE (7,10,N) EMOTIONS (8,6,SE)
FEELINGS (5,3,S) HEART (6,5,NW)
HOPE (12,4,NE) PERSEVERANCE (12,12,W)
PERSONALITY (12,13,NW) PURITY (14,1,SW)
SHINE (5,13,W) WORDS (1,5,N)

My Amazing Family Word Search Solution

```
L + + + + Y D A D + + + + + R
O + + + L + + + + + R + + E +
V + + I + + + + + + E + L + +
E + M + + + + + + + H A + + +
+ A + + + S + + + + T + + + +
F + + + + + G + + I E + + + T
H O M E + + + N V + G + + + R
+ O + + + + + E I + O + + + A
M + + + + + S + P L T + + + D
+ N E R D L I H C E B + + + I
+ + + + + + + + + + T I + + T
+ + + + + + + + + + S S + I
+ Y + + + + + + + + + + + O
+ + O + + + + + + + + + + N
+ + + J + + + + + + + + + S
```

(Over, Down, Direction)
CHILDREN (9,10,W) DAD (9,1,W)
FAMILY (1,6,NE) HOME (1,7,E)
JOY (4,15,NW) LOVE (1,1,S)
MOM (3,7,SW) PETS (9,9,SE)
RELATIVES (15,1,SW) SIBLINGS (13,12,NW)
TOGETHER (11,9,N) TRADITIONS (15,6,S)

True Friend Word Search Solution

```
+ + + + + + + + D + L C + S L
+ + G + + + + N + U A + + I A
+ + N F + + I + F R + + + N Y
+ + I + U K + H I + + + + C O
+ + G + + N T N G + + + + E L
+ + A + + I G + + N + + + R +
+ + R + A T R U S T I N G E +
+ + U F P + + + + + + V + + +
+ + O + + A + + + + + + O + +
N I C E + + T + + + + + + L +
+ + N + + + + I + + + + + + +
+ + E + + + + + E + + + + + +
+ + + + + + + + + N + + + + +
+ + + + + + + + + + T + + + +
T S E N O H + + + + + + + + +
```

(Over, Down, Direction)
CARING (12,1,SW) ENCOURAGING (3,12,N)
FAITHFUL (4,8,NE) FUN (4,3,SE)
HONEST (6,15,W) KIND (6,4,NE)
LOVING (14,10,NW) LOYAL (15,5,N)
NICE (1,10,E) PATIENT (5,8,SE)
SINCERE (14,1,S) TRUSTING (6,7,E)